Love so Amazing

Love so Amazing

ROBERT MOYER

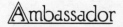

Ambassador

Love So Amazing
This edition 1990

First printed in 1936 as
"Christ in Isaiah Fifty-Three"

AMBASSADOR PRODUCTIONS LTD
Providence House
16 Hillview Avenue
Belfast BT5 6JR, UK.

37 Leaconfield Road,
Loughborough,
Leics. U.K. LE11 3SP

ISBN 0 907927 54 8

Printed in the United Kingdom by Ambassador Productions Ltd.

Foreword . . .

Isaiah 53 has been called "the evangelical heart of the Old Testament."

We believe that nowhere else in the Word will we find deeper, richer truth concerning the Messiah than in this prophecy. His sufferings and glory are foretold here with many details. "The sufferings and the exaltation of Christ are announced as clearly as if the prophet had stood at the foot of the Cross, and seen the Risen One" (Delitzsch).

The theme of Isaiah 53 is the greatest theme of the universe—Christ. The work of Isaiah 53 is the greatest work ever performed—redemption. The blessing of Isaiah 53 is the greatest blessing bestowed upon man—salvation.

The purpose of this book is to do exactly what Philip did in Acts 8 when he "preached unto him Jesus"—Jesus, Who is our Savior and Lord. May the results be the same as confessed by the eunuch when he said, "I believe."

These chapters are the result of long meditation on THE CHAPTER. Because they are human writings they must of necessity be imperfect, but, such as they are, we humbly lay them at the feet of our Lord, with the prayer that His blessing may be upon them unto the edification of His saints and the salvation of sinners.

"To Him who loves us and has freed us from our sins with His own blood . . . to Him be ascribed the glory and the power forever and ever. Amen" Revelation 1:5

Minneapolis, Minn.
June, 1936.

ROBERT L. MOYER.

Contents

★

Chapter I

His Marred Face

"Behold, my servant shall deal prudently, he shall be exalted and extolled, and be very high. As many were astonied at thee; his visage was so marred more than any man, and his form more than the sons of men: So shall he sprinkle many nations; the kings shall shut their mouths at him: for that which had not been told them shall they see; and that which they had not heard shall they consider" (Isaiah 52: 13-15).

"METHINKS Isaiah writes not a prophecy, but a Gospel," said Augustine. Manton said, "This portion of Scripture may rather be called the Gospel than the prophecy of Isaiah. It contains so ample and clear a discovery of Jesus Christ that one would rather account it historical than prophetical." Isaiah has been called the "Fifth Gospel." The meaning of the name Isaiah is "Salvation is of Jehovah." This gives us a key to the book, for here we have salvation not only for the Jew, but also for the Gentile. The person spoken of in this portion of Scripture is none other than the Messiah. In the eighth chapter of Acts in the record of the conversion of the royal sinner, Philip preached Jesus from this Scripture. He, as well as all others, must preach Jesus from this prophecy. It can be fulfilled by no other person. The generally accepted modern Jewish interpretation of this prophecy which makes it apply to the Jewish nation will not hold water. It will satisfy neither the intellect nor the heart of the one who studies it.

Honesty in dealing with it will prove it to be a teacher leading to Christ. A few years ago, in a conversation with the writer, a Hebrew believer testified that when he was in a Jewish school, studying to become a rabbi, his interest in Isaiah 53 led him to his Saviour. He said that in his study this Scripture seemed to grip him. His teachers tried to pass over it, but he asked many questions about it. The replies were evasive and unsatisfactory, but as he continued to study it, the Holy Spirit brought light and he came to know that the Person of Isaiah 53 was none other than Jesus, his own Messiah and Saviour.

The chapter division here is very poor. We all well know that the chapter divisions in the Bible are not divine, but human. In other words, they are man-made divisions. We are glad for these divisions when it comes to finding a certain place in Scripture, but too often these divisions divide truth, and cause us to lose the message of the Word. The fifty-third chapter of Isaiah should include chapter 52, verses 13 to 15. These three verses give us an introduction to, and summary of the teaching of the fifty-third chapter. Isaiah 53 is found in the second half of Isaiah, called by the rabbi, "The Book of Consolation." This second half of the book of Isaiah consists of the last twenty-seven chapters and has been described as the sublimest and richest portion of Old Testament revelation. David Baron calls it "The Prophetic Messianic Epic of the Old Testament." He says, "It is sublime in its very style and language, and wonderful in its comprehensiveness, anticipating, as it does, the whole order of the New Testament. It begins where the New Testament begins, with the ministry of John the Baptist—'the voice of him that crieth in the wilderness, prepare ye the way of the Lord'—and it ends where the New Testament ends, with the new heavens and a new earth wherein shall dwell righteousness (chapters 40:3-5; 65:17-20 and 66:22). The heart and climax of the whole prophecy is found in this brief section which we are now studying. It is a narrative of the sufferings of Christ and the glory that should follow.

His Introduction

Verse 13

This section starts: "Behold, my servant." God is introducing His Servant. He wants to direct the attention of all men to Him. When you find that word *behold*, mark it, for God is seeking to bring to your attention something of the utmost importance. Here in Isaiah when God uses that word, He wants to call our attention to His only begotten Son, Who came in the form of a Servant. God uses that word *behold* in other places in the Word to call attention to the same person. He says in Zechariah 9:9, "Behold thy king"; in Zechariah 6:12, "Behold the man"; in Isaiah 40:9, "Behold your God"; here in Isaiah 52:13, "Behold, my servant." It was not necessary to mention the Servant's name as in the case of "my servant Abraham," or "my servant Moses," for God never had but one perfect Servant. In Philippians 2 we read of Him: "He was in the form of God, yet He thought that equality with God was not a thing to be held on to, but emptied Himself and took upon Himself the form of a Servant." Then, when He was here upon earth, He said, "I came down from heaven not to do my will, but the will of Him that sent me." He said again, "My meat is to do the will of Him that sent me"; and these are His words, "I delight to do Thy will, O God." So God says here, "Behold Him in Whom my soul delighteth." We believe it important to emphasize the fact that He was the Servant of Jehovah rather than the Servant of man. Being a servant of man will make a man a mere humanitarian and man needs more than humanitarianism. It is only the Servant of Jehovah Who will prove to be of real service to man in bringing him the message that meets his preeminent need, that of salvation.

3

God had no question as to the conduct of His Servant seven hundred years before He was born and so declared "that He should deal prudently," or the Revised Version says, "wisely." In Jeremiah 23:5 we read, "Behold the days come, saith Jehovah, that I will raise up unto David a righteous branch and a king shall reign and prosper (*deal wisely*), and shall exercise justice and judgment in the land." This means that the Servant of Jehovah shall deal wisely in carrying out the work which the Father gave Him to do. The word implies success as the result of a prudent plan. He shall so act throughout His mission as to secure the most complete success.

God also declares that His Servant shall be exalted and extolled, or lifted up, and shall be very high. This is the same expression used in chapter 6, verse 1, where Isaiah declares, "I saw also the Lord high and lifted up," yet that seems not to be enough to the prophet here, for he adds, "He shall be glorified exceedingly," or "exalted exceedingly." That undoubtedly means that the highest place of honor shall be His. In Philippians 2:9 there is a "wherefore." He has emptied Himself to become a Servant, and as a Servant He has become obedient unto death, "*Wherefore* God also hath highly exalted Him." In Ephesians 1:21 we read that "He is set down on the right hand of God *far* above all principality, and power, and might, and dominion, and everything that is named." The natural man likes to exalt himself. He is insignificant, and yet he likes to be lifted up. Here was One Who was equal with God, yet took on the form of a Servant, and "He who humbleth himself shall be exalted."

His Sufferings
Verse 14

In the fourteenth verse we go from the high mountain peak of His exaltation and glorification way down into the valley of His suffering and shame. "Many were astonied at Thee," that is, astonished or

4

amazed at Him. The words which follow should be in parentheses, as we find them in the revised version, "His visage was so marred more than any man, and His form more than the sons of men." These words tell us why many were astonished at Him. It was because of His humiliation. It was because of the disfigurement of face and form. He was so marred that there was no trace of the grace and beauty which belonged to face and figure. Dr. Scofield says the literal rendering is terrible: "So marred from the form of man was His aspect that His appearance was not that of a son of man"—that is, not human. This is the effect of the brutalities to which He was subjected. Someone has said that the prophet, when writing this, was sitting at the foot of the Cross of Calvary to see the Redeemer as He hung upon the accursed tree after He had been buffeted, and crowned with thorns, and smitten, and scourged, and crucified, when the face was covered with bruises and with gore, and His frame and features distorted with agony. There is suffering here! Psalm 22 gives us that graphic picture of our Saviour, pierced in hands and feet, bones out of joint, His broken heart like melted wax within Him, the cry "Forsaken!" wrung from His lips. Surely the universe has never seen another such spectacle of misery as it saw when our Lord was crucified. We believe that Dr. F. B. Meyer was looking upon that cross, and that the pulse beat of his heart was in his pen when he wrote, "O King of suffering and sorrow, Monarch of the marred face! None has ever approached Thee in the extremity of Thy grief; we bow the knee, and bid Thee 'All hail.' We are conquered by Thy tears and woes; our hearts are enthralled; our souls inspired; our lives surrendered to Thy disposal for the execution of purposes which cost Thee so dear."

We believe that the Holy Spirit is limited by the limitations of human speech as He tries to bring to us a picture of the sufferings of our Saviour which

5

were the cost of our salvation. Oh, that God would cause us to see, and break our hearts for sin, our sin, which was the cause of it all.

His Glories
Verse 15

Verse 14, which tells of the marred Christ, begins with the little word *as*, and verse 15 begins with *so*. "So shall He sprinkle many nations; the kings shall shut their mouths at Him." The Septuagint version has "So shall many nations marvel at Him." Rotterham translates this, "The more doth He startle many nations; before Him have kings closed their mouths." The phrase "kings shall shut their mouths at Him" means because of Him (that is, shut the mouth in astonishment and reverence), so we have in verse 14, "because of His humiliation," and in verse 15, "because of His glorification." Many people were astonished at Him when He came the first time. Many nations will be astonished when He comes the second time. His mouth was shut when He came the first time when they put Him on the Cross. Their mouths will be shut when He comes the second time, when God puts Him on the throne. Men may today open their mouths against Him. They may revile Him, and blaspheme Him, and reject Him. They may today cry, "Away with Him, crucify Him," but the time will come when they shall be dumb before Him with awe. "The heathen may rage, and the kings of the earth set themselves, and the rulers take counsel together against the Lord, and against His Anointed, saying, 'Let us break their bands asunder, and cast away their cords from us'" (Psalm 2:1-3); but the time will come when the kings of the earth will be subject to Him, and reverence Him, and prostrate themselves before Him, for He shall come as King of kings and Lord of lords in that day when a voice from heaven shall cry, "The Lord God Omnipotent reigneth." Hear God's Word, Isaiah 49:7:

6

"Thus saith the Lord, the Redeemer of Israel,
    and His Holy One,
To Him Whom man despiseth,
To Him Whom the nation abhorreth,
To a Servant of rulers,
Kings shall see and arise,
Princes also shall worship,
Because of Jehovah that is faithful,
And the Holy One of Israel,
Who hath chosen thee."

Again God speaks of a time when He shall have
dominion over the whole earth:

"He shall have dominion from sea to sea,
And from the river unto the ends of the earth.
They that dwell in the wilderness shall bow•before
    Him,
And His enemies shall lick the dust.
The kings of Tarshish and of the isles shall bring
    presents,
The kings of Sheba and Seba shall offer gifts:
Yea, all kings shall fall down before Him;
All nations shall serve Him" (Psalm 72:8-11).

There are authorities who believe the word *sprinkle*
in verse 15 is the proper translation in this text and
that the word *so* corresponds with the *as* of the preceding verse, meaning that as His sorrow was intense, so shall His redeeming power be large, as if
the one were a recompense for the other. This may
be right, for there were in the economy of Israel two
kinds of sprinkling, both of which may be referred
to here. The first was a sprinkling of the blood
upon the Mercy Seat. This took place once a year
on Israel's greatest day of the year, the great Day
of the Atonement. On this day Israel approached
God through the priest, and the blood which was
sprinkled upon the Mercy Seat indicated the expiation of sin by sacrifice. On that day their sin was
put away. There was also in Israel a sprinkling

of water both in the case of the Levite and in the case of the leper. The Levite, sprinkled with water, signified a man cleansed for divine service. The leper, sprinkled with water, indicated a sinner cleansed from the pollution of his sin. Both of these sprinklings are typical of the work accomplished by our Lord and Saviour. He has made expiation for sin, and provided cleansing for the unclean. The blood sprinkled on the Mercy Seat was Godward; the water sprinkled on the leper was manward. Thus the work of Christ has the double aspect of blood shed as God's atoning act *for* us, the cleansing as God's purifying act *in* us. Both of these blessings are in Christ and in their individual application both cover the same ground. All who are pardoned are cleansed.

> "Rock of Ages, cleft for me,
> Let me hide myself in Thee;
> Let the water and the blood,
> From Thy riven side which flowed,
> Be of sin the double cure,
> Save me from its guilt and power."

We see the wondrous grace of God in that through the Servant He has made provision for the cleansing of many nations. Salvation is not for the Jew only, but also for the Gentile. "Divine mercy covers with its sheltering wing penitents in all the nations." The great sacrifice of Calvary's Cross has opened the door of salvation to "whosoever will". The last part of the fifteenth verse may be a little difficult. It reads, "For that which had not been taught them shall they see, and that which they had not heard, shall they consider." We believe that this looks off to the time when all the nations and their kings shall hear and understand the Gospel. The Pulpit Commentary says, "They will learn the acts of Christ's humiliation, sufferings, death, resurrection, and ascension into heaven—events that had never entered into the heart of man to conceive and of which, therefore, no tongue had ever spoken." There are multitudes today who do not know of God's love for a lost world and of the gift of His Son that they might be saved. We believe that as Christians we are responsible to carry this message into the uttermost parts of the earth, especially to those sections that have never yet been evangelized.

As Christians we know that the only hope for this world is the coming again of our great God and Saviour, Jesus Christ, when He shall take unto Himself the kingdoms of the world to reign and rule in righteousness. For this we long; for this we pray.

When Queen Victoria had just ascended her throne, she went, as is the custom of royalty, to hear "The Messiah" rendered. She had been instructed as to her conduct by those who knew, and was told that she must not rise when the others stood at the singing of the Hallelujah Chorus. When that magnificent chorus was being sung and the singers were shouting: "Hallelujah! Hallelujah! Hallelujah! for the Lord God Omnipotent reigneth," she sat with great difficulty. It seemed that she would rise in spite of the custom of kings and queens, but finally when they came to the part of the chorus where with a shout they proclaimed Him King of kings and Lord of lords, suddenly the young queen arose and stood with bowed head, as if she would take her crown from her head and cast it at His feet.

> "Ye chosen seed of Israel's race
> Ye ransomed from the fall,
> Hail Him Who saves you by His grace
> And crown Him Lord of all."

Chapter II

His Masked Personality

*"Who hath believed our report? and to whom
is the arm of the Lord revealed? For he shall
grow up before him as a tender plant, and as
a root out of a dry ground: he hath no form
nor comeliness; and when we shall see him,
there is no beauty that we should desire him"*
(Isaiah 53:1, 2).

THAT the personal pronouns *he, his,* and *him*
of this chapter refer to Christ is settled for
all time by Acts 8, in which Philip preaches
Jesus. Acts 8 also makes clear the fact that
Isaiah 53 has an application to the Gentiles as well
as to the Jews.

The introduction to chapter 53 is found in Isaiah
52:13-15. In this introduction we have summarized
the wonderful story of the self-humiliation and the
vicarious suffering of the Servant of God, who went
even unto death for our salvation. Following His
humiliation we have His exaltation and glorification.

Prophesied Unbelief

Verse one of chapter 53 opens with two great
questions: "Who hath believed our report?" and
"To whom is the arm of the Lord revealed?" These
questions have reference to the great truth of the
humiliation and the exaltation of the Servant of
Jehovah which Isaiah has just set forth. These
questions are put into the mouth of the prophet Isaiah although the questioner is really God Himself.
This fact adds an element of greatness, since a ques-

tion asked by Jehovah is of much more importance than one asked by a prattling babe. In the word *report* we have the thought of *words*, while in the phrase *arm of the Lord* we have the thought of *works*. The arm of the Lord is the emblem of Divine strength. In Isaiah 59:1, Israel appeals to it, "Put on thy strength, O Arm of Jehovah," and in Isaiah 52:10 we read, "Jehovah hath made bare His holy arm in the sight of all the nations, and all the ends of the earth shall see the salvation of our God." Hence we are right in saying that in the first verse we have set forth the words and the works of God. Our Lord Jesus Christ quoted this verse in John 12:38 when He was met by rejection. In the preceding verse (37) we read that although He had done many signs before them, yet they believed not on Him, and following this, He brought to them the message of Isaiah. In the fifteenth chapter of John, verse 11, He said, "Believe me"— that is, "Believe my words"—and then He went on to say, "Or else believe me for the very works' sake," but these people to whom He came believed neither His words nor His works. This is the unbelief that is prophesied by Isaiah. The answer to the question, "Who hath believed?" is implied. Very few believed. Even His own disciples were filled with unbelief, for when He told them plainly that He must go to Jerusalem and suffer many things, *and* be crucified, and buried, and rise again, Peter tried to dissuade Him, and said, "Not so, Lord."

Indeed, it seems that there was only one person in all Israel who did believe, and that was Mary, who anointed Him unto His burial.

But we may go further than this, and say that the "Arm of the Lord" is more than an emblem of Divine power—it is Jesus Christ Himself. The poets and prophets often speak of *the holy arm, the glorious arm, the redeeming arm* of Jehovah. God said to Moses, in connection with the redemption of Israel, "I will redeem them with a stretched-out arm."

11

In the song of salvation by the sea, Israel recognized that it was the stretched-out Arm of Jehovah Who made a path in the depths by which His ransomed might pass through the sea. God's Arm piled up the waters of the Jordan, and overthrew the walls of Jericho. God's Arm stopped the sun for Joshua, and wielded the sword for Gideon. The exploits of Hebrew story are attributed to the Arm of Jehovah. Then came the day when Jesus Christ became the embodiment of the power of God—the out-stretched Arm of Jehovah. One old writer has said, "In the Servant of Jehovah Who is depicted in this prophecy the redeeming Arm of Jehovah manifests itself, or personifies itself. The Messiah Himself is the outstretched Arm of Jehovah," and the message concerning Him is "the power of God unto salvation." The Arm became flesh, and in Him God did His greatest work.

Note that the question indicates that the Arm of the Lord must be *revealed*. Our Lord asked, "Whom do men say that I the Son of Man am?" They answered: "Some say that Thou art John the Baptist; some, Elias; and others, Jeremias, or one of the prophets." Then He said to them, "But whom say *ye* that I am?" Simon Peter answered and said, "Thou art the Christ, the Son of the living God." It was then that our Lord said what is always true: "Flesh and blood hath not revealed it unto thee, but my Father which is in heaven." We conclude this section by remarking that it is God's part to reveal and it is man's part to believe.

The Cause of Unbelief

No doubt the second verse of this chapter explains the reason for the unbelief that met our Lord Jesus at His coming. The Arm of the Lord was concealed by the lowliness, obscurity, and sorrow of His appearance. The personality of the Messiah was masked by His form of the servant. The second verse beginning with "For" gives the reason why so few believed on Him: "For He shall grow up before Him as a tender plant, and as a root out of a dry ground."

Let us look first at the "dry ground." The dry ground speaks of His surroundings. It describes the state of the enslaved people in the midst of whom He was born, and among whom He must dwell and develop. It declares an ancestry that was corrupt to the last degree. It tells of the deadness and dryness of sin of the whole human race. The world and mankind became "dry ground" through the fall of Adam. The blight of sin passed over mankind, and wherever sin reached, death reached. In Adam all sinned. The father of all men sinned, and all his family sinned in him, for who can bring a clean thing out of an unclean? No one! God said to Eve, "I will greatly multiply thy sorrow and thy conception; in sorrow thou shalt bring forth children" (Gen. 3:16). She brought forth children, children of sin, children of sorrow, children of shame, children of disobedience, children of wrath, children of death. So "by one man sin entered the world, and death by sin." Sin entered into the world, into our spirit, into our soul, into our body, into the very stronghold of our life, so that our life became death. "And so death passed upon all men, for that all have sinned." So dry was the world, so dry was the human race, that there could be no hope apart from the visitation of Jehovah.

Out of this dry land, arid land, parched by the drought and heat of sin, sprang a tender plant. Sometimes the word translated "tender plant" is used of infants, and means "suckling," as in the words, "Out of the mouth of babes and sucklings hast Thou ordained strength." In a horticultural sense it is sometimes used figuratively for the tender twig upon a tree, or for a root-sprout, or suckling—"sucker" we sometimes call it. That means that in this verse the birth and early growth of our Lord is likened to the springing forth of a root shoot or sapling from the root or stump, after the proud cedar of the kingdom of Judah had been felled. The Davidic monarchy had been felled under the axe of God's judgment. Out of the root of the decayed house of David comes the tender plant, struggling out of the dry ground.

Every plant owes much to the ground in which it grows, for there it gets its life and nourishment. But our Saviour certainly derived nothing from the dry ground from which He sprang. He derived nothing from his natural descent. He derived no assistance from His own nationality. He derived nothing from the day in which He lived. His people were sinners, His day one of corruption. There was nothing in either to nourish spiritual life. This plant had a hidden life. It struck its roots far out to draw its sap from the bosom of God. It was the life of God that circulated through its stem and leaves. That is why the tender plant sprang up, and the root shot forth its shoots when the ground was utterly dry. It had a life not found among men, who were dead, nor among angels, who stand by grace. That plant was the One to Whom the Father hath given to have life in Himself, even as He hath life in Himself. That life was a life that could reach farther than death, as we shall see later. By all this we mean that He Who is Spirit and Life became the partaker of flesh and blood derived from Adam; but that He might be free from the taint of Adam's sin, He was not conceived as others. He was conceived of the Holy Ghost and born of the Virgin Mary, that He might be one of us in nature, and yet "holy, harmless, undefiled, and separate from sinners." He was separate; He alone was without sin. Here He differed from us, but in all other things He was like us. He was formed as we all are formed, born as we are born. He grew as we grow, lived as we live, and died as we die. Thus was He identified with the human race, but because He came as a "tender plant" instead of a plant of renown they did not believe on Him. Because He was a sprout from

14

the root of a tree which had been cut down, instead of a cedar which lifted its boughs in majesty, they did not believe on Him. So the Arm of the Lord was veiled.

"He shall grow up before Him"—that is, before Jehovah, Who sent Him. He grew up under Jehovah's watchful eye and fostering care. He was a babe on a mother's breast. He opened wide His eyes to look wonderingly upon an unknown world. He learned to talk. He indulged in play. He went to work. He grew from a babe into a child, from a boy into a man. He "grew up" by a natural human growth. He increased in wisdom and stature. Jesus Christ was a man—nay, THE MAN. He was more than man, of course. He was the God-Man—not, as some one has said, the man-God, but the God-Man. Wonder of wonders! He Who in His humanity was the shoot from David was in His Deity the root of David. He was Divine, and David sprang from Him, but He was human, and He sprang from David. He is "the root and the offspring of David" (Rev. 22:16). It was in relation to His humanity that we have the thought of Jehovah's tender care. He was under the special providences of God. Witness the flight into Egypt, when God warned Joseph in a dream concerning the danger under which the babe rested. Time and again attempts were made upon His life, but the Father's protecting love was about Him. None could lay hand upon Him until His hour was come.

He "grew up" before God, not before the public. He was nurtured amid the quiet of devotion and godliness. Through thirty years He was "before God"—years called "the silent years at Nazareth." Only once was the silence broken, when as a lad of twelve He declared that He must be about His Father's business. When He was thirty, He appeared in public to accomplish the work which the Father gave Him to do.

The remaining words of this verse which explain

the reason for the prophesied unbelief read, "He hath no form nor comeliness; and when we shall see Him there is no beauty that we should desire Him." What does this mean? Was not our Lord personally attractive? Surely He must have been. His beauty set forth in the Word is moral and spiritual, and this is real beauty. The silence of the Scripture on the appearance of the Lord is most instructive. The intent of the Word is to give us His spirit rather than His form, and to lift us up to an appreciation of His inward, rather than His outward glory. As Clemance says, "Though we know not what the face of Christ was like, we are sure it must have beamed with benevolence, must have manifested sympathy, must have been marked by earnestness, purity, decision, and holy self-surrender. All these, expressed in the face, must have disclosed a beauty of the very highest type"; yet to the eyes of many there was no beauty that they should desire Him.

Rotherham translates the foregoing words as follows: "He had neither beauty nor majesty; when we beheld Him there was nothing to behold that we should desire Him." Probably He was not strikingly handsome physically, as the first Adam, or as His great ancestor, David; and He had no majesty. He came with no pomp of regal state, with no insignia of royalty such as the world admires. There was nothing of the show and glitter which attract the earth-born soul. He would be "all glorious within," though destitute of brightness and glory to those without. Israel would have welcomed a plumed and mail-clad warrior riding forth to deliver them from the oppression of Rome, but He came as the meek and lowly One, and so they did not desire Him. They wanted some one like Saul, who stood head and shoulders above the people, a king after man's eyes instead of One after God's heart. Because He came without outward imperialism, He did not have their admiration. He was *meek*; they thought He was *weak*. He did not look like a Monarch, although

16

He was a Monarch—the Monarch with the masked personality. He did not assume royal splendor nor robes of state, and men turned away from the thought that the deepest lowliness was a manifestation of God. The finger of scorn was pointed at Him. He was misunderstood. One of His own denied Him; one betrayed Him. When the depth of His humiliation was upon Him, they forsook Him and fled. Men cried, "Away with Him!" "Crucify Him!" They led Him away to Calvary to crucify Him. There the Arm of the Lord was nailed to the tree; and when men stood about the Cross to look at the marred face and tortured form of the Saviour ("His visage was so marred more than any man, and His form more than the sons of men," Isaiah 52:14), certainly there was no beauty that they should desire Him. But in that hour of His deepest humiliation, the Arm of the Lord was stretched forth to do His greatest work. Israel looked for the Arm of the Lord to overthrow the thrones of rival nations, that their throne might be established, but now the Arm of the Lord, pierced through with nails, is stretched forth in infinite love to lift men into an eternal salvation. But still the veil is upon the heart, the Arm of the Lord unrevealed, the report not believed.

Present Day Unbelief

With this prophecy before us, we ought not to be surprised that even to this day the Gospel is veiled. The prophet said it would be so, and Paul declared that "The god of this age hath blinded the minds of men which believe not, lest the light of the glorious gospel of Christ....should shine into them." Sin has so stopped the ears and hearts of men, and has so blinded their eyes, that they can neither hear the report, nor see the revelation. The "report" comes to us today in the Gospel. The Gospel is "good tidings" —that Christ died for our sins, and that He was buried and that He was raised again from the dead. It is the good tidings by which we are saved (I Cor.

15:1-4). It announces a salvation without money and without price. It is "life and immortality brought to light." It is the ministry of reconciliation. It offers the Arm of the Lord as an indwelling Presence in the life, that we through Him might have every blessing for this world and that which is to come. It throws open the gates of heaven and offers us eternal joys and glories as the children of God. Yea, "As it is written, Eye hath not seen, nor ear heard, neither have entered into the heart of man, the things which God hath prepared for them that love Him. But God hath revealed them unto us by His Spirit"—but only through and in the Gospel.

It is true that the Gospel announces the wrath of God, but, thank God, it tells us that that wrath was borne by Christ when He was nailed to the tree to die in our stead, that He might be made unto us "wisdom, righteousness, sanctification, and redemption."

The Gospel is announced by God. It is written in the Blood of Christ. It is sealed with the Holy Spirit. It is a savour of life unto life, or death unto death. It will result in salvation, or damnation.

"Who hath believed our report? and to whom is the arm of the Lord revealed?"

We must put that question to ourselves now, or it will be put to us in the judgment day. Have I believed the report—the Gospel? Has the Arm of the Lord been revealed to me? Remember that faith is an individual act. Faith must accept the report. To faith the Arm of the Lord will be revealed. Remember that faith is "the substance of things hoped for, the evidence of things not seen." Again we say, the report is the Gospel; the effect of believing it is salvation. The Arm of the Lord is Jesus Christ, His Son and Word, and His revelation is eternal life. *"This is life eternal that they might know Thee, the only true God, and Jesus Christ Whom Thou hast sent."* Not to believe the report is damnation. To *lack* the revelation is eternal death. *"He that believeth on the Son hath everlasting life, and he that believeth not the Son shall not see life, but the wrath of God abideth on him."*

Let us ask once more, have *you* believed the report of the holy and blessed God? *"He that believeth not God hath made Him a liar; because he believed not the record that God gave of His Son"* (I John 5:10). Has the Arm of the Lord been revealed to you? Have you a real Saviour, in whom you believe? Has a real, living Arm been made known to you? Is it an Arm upon which you really lean? Is it an Arm that was stretched out in mercy, and that poured in the oil and wine of salvation? Is it an Arm that holds you, and draws you back from temptation, and carries you, and cherishes you? Is it an Arm that wipes your tears, and soothes your pains? Is it an Arm that is stretched forth in you for life and service so that "you can do all things through Christ Who strengtheneth you?" Is the Lord Jesus, the Arm of the Lord, real to *you*?

We beseech you, go to the garden of Gethsemane and see the bloody sweat; go to the Cross of Calvary and see the marred Face. Stand at Golgotha, the place of a skull, and see the unspeakable agony and suffering caused by the weight and judgment of your sins, and mine. Say it! "He loved *me*, and gave Himself for *me*."

Lord! tear the veil away from men's hearts that they may see that sight and live forever.

Chapter III

His Manifold Sorrows

"He is despised and rejected of men; a man of sorrows and acquainted with grief: and we hid as it were our faces from Him; He was despised and we esteemed Him not" (Isaiah 53:3).

"HE WAS despised and rejected of men." With this verse Handel opens the second part of his great oratorio, "The Messiah." It is said that at this point in its composition, Handel was found with his head upon the table, weeping.

Rejected

"He was despised and rejected of men." Who? The Incarnate God. The Servant of Jehovah here rises to the full stature of an individual, and that individual none other than the Lord Jesus Christ, our Saviour and Israel's Messiah—yea, more, King of kings and Lord of lords, the destined Monarch of the whole earth.

"He was despised and rejected of men." This, alas! is still the case. The few who have received Him would weep with Handel, but by the many He is either ignored or abhorred.

"He is (better rendered *was*) despised and rejected of men." This sentence, especially the latter phrase, "rejected of men," has been variously rendered. "His form was dishonored, and failing beyond that of men"; "the most unworthy among men"; "the meanest of men"; "shunned of men"; "He was despised and the last of men"; "He was less than man, the most abject of men"; "One from Whom all men shrink." Cocceius, Delitzsch, and others favor "wanting in men," that is, having no respectable men with Him to support Him with their authority. "The chief men of His nation who towered above the multitude, the great men of this world, withdrew their hands from Him: He had none of the men of any distinction at His side." Yet no matter what the rendering, the purport of these words remains practically the same; there is the same solemn melancholy, the same awful sadness. They set forth the terrible consequences of judging after the sight of the eyes and the outward appearance. Israel expected their Messiah to come in majesty and power. They looked to Him to vanquish all their enemies, "to bind their kings with chains, their nobles with links of iron." They expected to be the head of a new creation, its kings and priests, the objects of reverence, service, and praise to all the subject kingdoms of the earth. They had a certain right to expect this, of course, for the prophet had foretold the glories and the triumphs of their Messiah. His name was to be called "Wonderful," "Counsellor," "The Mighty God," "The Everlasting Father," "The Prince of Peace," "Emmanuel," or "God With Us." "Of the increase of His government and peace" there was to be no end. He was to "bring forth judgment to the Gentiles."

But there was another aspect of His coming—a dark aspect—revealed by Isaiah in language that could scarcely be mistaken, such as we have in this fifty-third chapter. His earthly life was to be such as best would be summed up in these words: "He was despised and rejected of men; a Man of sorrows and acquainted with grief." What are the facts? The birth of Jesus in Bethlehem was in poverty and like that of any other man. His circumcision was like that of any other Jewish child. His name was a common name. He lived for thirty years in subjection to His mother and Joseph, and even when

21

He entered upon His ministry, the fact that He had never been taught in the schools, that He had been brought up in Nazareth, and that He was known as "the carpenter's son" led many to despise Him. The finger of scorn was pointed at Him because His birth was misunderstood. He was careful to declare that He came not of Himself, and did nothing of Himself. He gathered His disciples, one here, another there, from the lowly orders of society. He paid tribute and custom. He showed respect to every constituted authority. He said nothing about the rights of the people or the claims of the Jewish race. He endured the contradiction of sinners. When He was reviled He reviled not again, and when He suffered, He threatened not. With meekness He bore insult and injury. Out of His own chosen band of twelve, one sold Him, another denied Him, and finally when the depth of His humiliation was approaching they all forsook Him and fled. He was as one with whom men had ceased to do. Instead of binding Rome's Caesar to His chariot wheels, He Himself was bound by Rome, and led like a lamb to the slaughter. His crown was of thorns, and His scepter only reed. His form was worn with watching and anguish, and His face, "marred more than any man's," was covered with "shame and spitting" and blood. He bowed to every oppression, submitted meekly to every indignity, and finally died in great agony. There was no beauty, or majesty that they should desire Him. "He was despised and rejected of men." The depth of contempt is set forth in Isaiah 49:7: "Him Whom man despiseth, Him Whom the nation abhorreth, a servant of rulers." Down through all the centuries that hatred and abhorrence have continued.

The hatred of the Jew against Him was, and is, intense and mysterious. David Baron, a saved Israelite, wrote: "I have known personally most amiable, lovable characters among the Jews; but as soon as the name 'Jesus' was mentioned, a change came

22

over their countenances, and they would fall into a passion of anger. In the course of my missionary experiences these past thirty-five or forty years, how often has it been my lot to witness some of my people almost mad with rage—clenching their fists, gnashing their teeth, and spitting on the ground at the very mention of the Name which to the believer 'is as ointment poured forth'! Israel's attitude to our Lord may be gathered also from their literature. In the filthy legends about Him in the Talmud and more modern productions, the very names by which He is called are blasphemous. The precious name, 'Yeshua' (Jesus, Saviour) has been changed into 'Yeshu', made up of initial letters which mean, 'Let His name and His memory be blotted out.' The Holy One Who knew no sin nor was guile found in His mouth is often styled 'the Transgressor'; and another term frequently in the mouth of the Jews is 'Tolui' (the hanged one), which is equivalent to 'the accursed one.' There are also other hateful designations, such as 'Ben Stada', or 'Ben Pandera', which imply blasphemies not only against Him, but against her who is 'blessed among women'! Israel's blind hatred of the Messiah does not stop short at His person, or His virgin mother, but extends to His words and works......His works are still ascribed to witchcraft and Beelzebub."

This hatred is incomprehensible. The mystery of it is set forth in the words of our Lord: "They hated Me without a cause." Is it any wonder that He is a "Man of sorrows and acquainted with grief"?

Grieved

His was the saddest life ever lived. Our sorrows and griefs are only a shadow, and gone like a painful dream in comparison to His. He was a Man of sorrows—not a man with a sorrow. He was a Man of sorrows—not necessarily a sorrowful man, although we never read that "Jesus laughed," while we do read that "Jesus wept." There is reference to the fact that He "rejoiced", and we know that He had the perfect rest that comes through perfect trust in the Father. We believe, however, that the lost condition of the human race was ever upon His heart—this was the overwhelming burden of His life. What a burdened life it was, this earth life of our Lord!

He was a Man, but those who see in Him only the Man, can find very little comfort in the fact of His humanity. What hope can a sinner find in a man who confirms with an oath that He is the Son of God (Matt. 26:64), and knows that it is a lie? Christ is more than man, for He is all that He claimed to be— He is God become Man for man's sake. We cannot, with our limited capacities, comprehend the essence of the mighty God, but we can take hold of Him as He clothes Himself in our nature. In His human garb He came very near to us. As the second Man and the last Adam He patiently bore the death incurred by the first Adam, and thus through death became the life of a new humanity that believes on Him. He Who would have been distant to us as mere God, and useless to us as mere man, unites in Himself Divinity and humanity to become our wonderful Saviour.

But Christ is not only this wonderful Man—He is a Man of sorrows and acquainted with grief. "Man of sorrows" is really "Man of pains", the Hebrew idiom denoting "sorrow of heart in all its forms", a man whose chief distinction was that His life was one of constant, painful endurance. He was acquainted with grief. The word "grief" might be translated "sickness", but certainly the thought is not that He had a sickly body by nature, nor that He fell "from one disease into another", but rather that He was wounded mentally, as this word is used in Jeremiah 6:7 and 10:19. The thought here emphasized is that sorrow and grief were the characteristics of our Saviour, and, as another has said: "The chief causes of His sorrow and grief were not personal ills, or physical pain. They were heart sorrow and grief of soul."

He was a Man of sorrows because He was sinless.

He was, not only in act, but in nature, without sin, and the One with a sinless nature could not come into contact with sin without being filled with sorrow and grief. Sin has blunted us, and we do not feel its touch as He did. Some of us have lived in haunts of vice without disgust, where others would have been filled with horror; but think of the agony sin must have caused Him Whose nature is infinitely purer than the most refined nature of man. In John 2:24 we read that "He knew what was in Man," which means that He could see sin where we could never see it. We believe that the culmination of His sorrow came in the agony of Gethsemane.

He was a Man of sorrows because He was sympathetic.

Disease and distress, poverty and bereavement become common things with us. We are likely to become hardened, somehow, in the presence of the sorrows of others, but not so with Him. He was tender toward others. He felt with them and suffered with them. All men's sorrows were His sorrows. He wept with them that wept. He knew the hearts of men. Possibly if we knew the sorrows in the hearts of men we would have no rest tonight. He knew. They weighed upon His spirit as a heavy burden.

He was a Man of sorrows because He was solitary.

He moved among men but He was not of them. It is possible to be in a throng of men and still be lonely. He was solitary because He was sinless. His best friends failed to understand Him and appreciate Him. He stood before Pilate with no one to speak a word in His defense. He stood before Herod with no one to protest the indignities to which He was subjected. He was alone when they mocked

Him, and spit in His face, and crowned Him with thorns. He was lonely in His shame when He was made a curse for us. Alone upon the cross He hung —forsaken by man, forsaken by God.

He was a Man of sorrows because He was shunned.

His love was never recognized. What sharper pang does earth know, humanly speaking, than unrequited love? The heart has not upon earth a more cruel anguish than love centering and consuming itself upon some object and being rejected. I have read of a mother who shut herself in from the world for nineteen years to nurse a simple-minded son who never recognized her or called her mother. When a friend spoke to her about the sacrifice she was making for this boy she replied: "Oh, I have waited all these years for the slightest recognition, and if he would but call me 'Mother' once, I would be fully repaid for it all." But, oh, how long He has been rejected. "He was in the world, and the world was made by Him, and the world knew Him not." "He came unto His own, and His own received Him not." In the hours of His passion, when He was suffering and dying for men, He was still rejected, with scorn and contempt, and crucified instead of Barabbas. Undoubtedly in His death He saw countless numbers for whom He died despise and reject Him. Though He offered every blessing to men, they multiplied their insults against Him, the only Saviour, the only Life; and preferred their sins with all the consequences, to their God.

"It was the rejection which He was experiencing, and was to experience until the end, that went like the two-edged sword into His soul, wrung from Him the great bloody sweat, covered His eyes with the blackness of death, extorted that awful outcry of utter astonishment and desolation."

He was a Man of sorrows because He was the sin-offering.

26

His deep sense of human sin culminated in His sacrifice for it. Sorrow and grief have their origin in sin. The Son of God is without sin, but He was made in the likeness of sin's flesh that He might be made sin for us. He took unto Himself all the consequences of sin in all its breadth, length, height, and depth. All the sins of men from the first man to the last man pierced Him through and slew Him. Every cruel heel lifted up against Him from first to last stamped them into His heart, until it broke with the anguish. He "tasted death for every man", and the cup of death from which He drank was filled with all the woes of men and with all the wrath of God.

Ignored

"We hid, as it were, our faces from Him." The Revised Version reads: "As One from whom men hide their faces He was despised." Rotherham renders it: "Like One from whom the face is hidden," while Moffatt gives it as "One from whom men turn with shuddering." The Pulpit Commentary states that it should be rendered literally as "There was as it were the hiding of the face from Him."

There are some who suppose the hiding of *God's* face to be intended. This is the teaching of Clemance, who writes: "This phrase is often interpreted as if it indicated that men would hide their faces from Him; but the phrase 'the hiding of the face' denotes, in Scripture usage, an act on God's part, not on man's. We take the meaning of this clause to be this: 'It was as if God's face were hidden from Him.' Not only would earth be arrayed against Him, but it would be as if even Heaven had left Him to the mercy of His foes." We may truly say that in the awful hours of darkness when our Lord was on the cross the face of God was hidden from Him, but the context of this third verse of Isaiah 53 describes the treatment of the Servant of Jehovah by His fellow men, making the meaning in the Authorized Version preferable. *Men* turned their faces from Him.

The margin of the Authorized Version presents another thought in "He hid, as it were, *His* face from us." Lowth renders this clause: "He was as one hiding His face from us." There is a profitable application in this, also. He was despised and rejected of men, a Man of sorrows, and acquainted with grief, therefore our Saviour was as "One hiding His face from us." In the Orient in Bible days the face was covered for several reasons. The mourner hid his face, as in the case of David mourning as he went up Olivet. The leper was put without the camp and when he was approached by any of his brethren he must, according to the Levitical law, cover his lips and cry, "Unclean! unclean!" He was to utter this sad sentence against himself with a veiled face, as if unfit to meet the gaze of his clean brethren. "It is perhaps with a view to this precept that the Vulgate interprets the word 'stricken' in verse 4 by 'leprous,' understanding it to mean stricken with the excommunication of leprosy." Our blessed Lord hid His face in the sense that He was a mourner over the hardness and impenitence of those who rejected Him, and also in that He was to be dealt with as an unclean thing, and be made that of which leprosy is a striking type, even "made to be sin for us," pronounced not only unclean, but accursed.

If Christ did hide His face from men, remember that it was hidden from those who first hid their faces from Him. In hiding their faces from Him, they hid His face from them. In the hall of Caiaphas they blindfolded the Lord, and so covered His face, but the veil upon His face was only the veil upon their hearts. They covered His face because they loved darkness rather than light. The sin of the heart is this veil, and remember that sin may hide God's face forever.

We believe that while there is truth in the two foregoing interpretations, the true translation is given to us in the English versions, "We hid as it were our faces from Him." Men turned from Him as if it were impossible to endure Him. "Instead of meeting Him with a joyful gleam in their eyes responding to His grace and help, men turned away from Him—as one looks the other way to avoid the eye of a person whom he dislikes, or as one shrinks from an object of loathing," says Curloss.

This verse ends with the summing up: "He was despised, and we esteemed Him not." "He was despised"—this is a repetition, as if to intensify the abhorrence in which He was held. Then there is added the negative proposition, "We esteemed Him not," that is, reckoned Him of no account or worth. Luther forcibly expresses it: "We estimated Him at nothing." This is still the case. The few who have received Him would weep with Handel, but by the many He is either abhorred or ignored.

Chapter IV

His Mediatorial Mission

"Surely He hath borne our griefs, and carried our sorrows: yet we did esteem Him stricken, smitten of God, and afflicted. But He was wounded for our transgressions, He was bruised for our iniquities: the chastisement of our peace was upon Him; and with His stripes we are healed" (Isaiah 53:4, 5).

WE HAVE in these verses the very heart of the Gospel. We are now entering into a study of and a meditation on them. We are going to pause in spirit on Calvary's hill. We shall look upon our Savior crucified. We shall listen to the prophet as he tells of our Lord pierced and punished in our stead. Surely we are going to say with Spurgeon: "I have lost the power to doubt Him when I see those wounds."

Mission Accomplished By Our Savior

The word with which verse 4 begins, "Surely," is the "verily," or "amen," found so often on the lips of our Lord. It is a word that expresses the strongest affirmation, indicating that there must be not the slightest question as to the cause of the sufferings of the Mighty Monarch portrayed in this section of Isaiah, the Holy of Holies of the Book (52:13-53:12).

"Surely the griefs that He bore were our own;
The sorrows were ours that He carried."

The words which are here translated "griefs" and

"sorrows" might more literally be translated "sick-nesses" (or "diseases") and "pains." This verse is quoted in Matthew 8:16-17 in connection, not with the Cross, but with the miracles accomplished by our Lord before the Cross: "And when even was come, they brought unto Him many that were possessed with devils; and He cast out the spirits with a word, and healed all that were sick: that it might be fulfilled which was spoken by Isaiah the prophet, saying, Himself took our infirmities and bare our sick-nesses."

We do not believe with some that He was made all foul and loathsome disease when He hung upon the cross. He was our Sin-bearer. All sicknesses and pains, sorrows and griefs are caused by sin, and we believe that the prophet here uses a figure of speech called metonymy, by which he substitutes for sin the things brought about by sin. There is in this universe something far worse than sickness or pain, grief or sorrow, and that is SIN. All sorrows are the fruit of sin. Jesus Christ was our Sin-bearer. On Him the stroke of God's wrath fell in judgment on our sins. In that sense Christ's sufferings were the remedy for all the ills to which flesh is heir. He Who had power and authority on earth (Mark 2:10) to remove the *effect* of sin made Himself responsible for the *cause*. F. C. Jennings says, "He could not remove one single twinge of pain without, in due season, bearing the sin that caused the pain. And just as the feeblest groan, or a single teardrop is a testimony to the presence of sin, so the hushing of the groan, the drying of the tear is in the same way a testimony to the sin's being atoned for; and for that, nothing in the whole universe would avail but those sufferings during the last three hours upon the cross; and, as Matthew tells us, He did remove them so that the prophecy of Isaiah might be fulfilled, and fulfilled it was as in a shadow, but for the final true fulfillment we must look alone to the cross."

The mission of the Servant of Jehovah was to

accomplish full redemption for sin and all its consequences. Our salvation will reach its consummation in that day when our Lord Jesus Christ "shall fashion anew the body of our humiliation, that it may be conformed to the body of His glory." In that day the redemption of the whole man, spirit, soul, and body, will be completed. The healings which He performed when He was here on earth, not only served to certify that Jesus was the Christ, but also illustrated the spiritual healings which He came to bring.

The verbs used here, "borne" and "carried," signify "to take the debt of sin upon one's self, and carry it as one's own; i. e., to look at it and feel it as one's own; or, more frequently, to bear the punishment occasioned by sin; i. e., to make expiation for it, and, in any case in which the person is not himself the guilty person, to bear it in a mediatorial capacity for the purpose of making expiation for it," writes Delitzsch. We probably have the double notion here of sins borne vicariously, and sins borne or carried away. The terms are evidently drawn from the Mosaic law of sacrifice, a prominent feature in which is the substitution of the victim for the actual offender, so that the former bears the sins of the latter in expiation. Then there is the added feature of sins carried away, as recorded in Leviticus 16:22: "The goat shall bear upon him all their iniquities unto a land not inhabited." Thus the means and the effect of substitutionary sacrifice are set forth.

Misconceptions Entertained By Men

When Christ took upon Himself the crushing burden of our sins, blinded Israel considered His sufferings a punishment for the sins which He Himself had committed. They did not understand that He was bearing the sins of others in a mediatorial capacity. Hence they scoffed at Him, and reviled Him, even in His greatest agonies. This attitude is expressed in the words, "Yet we did esteem Him stricken, smitten of God, and afflicted." These words describe one suffering terrible punishment for sin. "Stricken" has the sense of a judicial affliction, as one afflicted with the hateful, shocking disease of leprosy, which was a direct Divine judgment for guilt (Lev. 13; II Chron. 26:18-21). This has been translated as "We thought Him to be a leper." Alexander declares that there was an old Jewish notion that the Messiah was to be a leper. The word "stricken" means "to strike heavily" in judgment. The word "smitten" gives us the idea of a rebel who has been defeated in his conflict against God, and who has been smitten with Divine judgment. The word "afflicted" means "humbled" or "one bowed down by suffering," and is used to describe one smitten down, humbled, crushed as the result of judgment upon sin. While we do not believe that our Lord was made a leper, we do know that He was made sin, and that He suffered the just judgment of God against our sins. It was then that the bitter cry pierced through the darkness: "Eli, Eli, lama sabacthani" (Matt. 27:46). "No rod that ploughed His flesh, no thorn that tore His brow, no nail that pierced His hands and feet could wring from Him one recorded groan. 'It needed greater agony, e'en than these, to force that cry.' What could that be? At the meridian hour man's gibes cease; and then the cloudless sun refuses to send down its light on that most solemn scene, whilst *my* sins (Will you not join with me, with bowed head, and eye not undimmed?) are on Him, and God, even His own God forsakes Him therefor, and stripes from His rod—compared with which the Roman rods were but as a caressing—are falling on Him. It was from this, and this alone, that His holy soul shrank, so that His sweat was as it were great drops of blood; and yet there, too, in that garden, it was but the shadow; *what, O what, must the substance have been?*" writes Jennings.

Meaning Set Forth By God

There might have been reason for the Jewish interpretation of the sufferings of Christ, had His career ended at the cross. Had His life terminated in that darkness, there could be no vindication from the charges laid against Him by His enemies. But Christ's career did not end at the cross. HE ROSE AGAIN. And when He was raised from the grave that resurrection vindicated Him gloriously from the charge that He was suffering for His own sins, for He was "declared to be the Son of God with power, according to the spirit of holiness, by the resurrection from the dead."

Isaiah tells us, in this fifth verse, that while the people misunderstood the sufferings of Christ, there was only one meaning to them, and that was that He bore the sins of others, and suffered in substitutionary sacrifice.

We know that the word "substitution" is found nowhere in Scripture, but the truth of substitution is found everywhere in it. Where will you find a better word to express the truth set forth in elementary form in the sacrifices and offerings of the Mosaic economy? If the ram on the altar in the place of Isaac be not substitution, what is it? What other word will so express the sublime conception brought to us in "He was wounded for our transgressions, He was bruised for our iniquities; the chastisement of our peace was upon Him; and with His stripes we are healed." If you say that this means no more than that their Messiah would be so grieved at them that they would in that way wound or bruise Him, take the far fuller and clearer expression: "The Lord hath laid on Him the iniquity of us all," which declares (not merely implies) that there was some appointment in heaven whereby the sins of all were laid upon Him. The world's sin was, as it were, rolled up into one vast burden, and made to light on Him. "His person was so Divinely

34

great that He *could* represent the world: His love was so vast that He *did*; He so identified Himself with sin and sinners that He 'was made to be sin for us'." This is substitution.

The words "transgressions," and "iniquities" mean practically the same. The first word means that we have crossed the boundary line between good and evil, and that we have gone completely over to the wrong side. This has been in violation of the Word, the way, the will of God. The second word "iniquities," means "to bend" or "to twist" and indicates that we have taken the crooked, winding way of our own will to walk "according to the course of this world," rather than to walk the straight path of righteousness. In the expression "the chastisement of our peace was upon Him," we have the same thought. He bore the chastisement, or punishment which leads to our peace. Van Orelli expresses it: "The punishment of our well-being; i. e., by the bearing of which, on His part, our peace or well-being is secured—was upon Him." He bore the burden of it in our stead, and because of the correction inflicted upon Him, we are reconciled to God. He made peace by the blood of His cross.

The fifth verse ends with "by His stripes we are healed." Let us not forget that this means that the people were not to be healed by their own suffering, but only through the Savior's voluntary submission to the Divine chastisement.

Just in passing, let us note these two blessed results from the substitutionary work of our Savior—peace and healing. We have peace with God because we are justified by the blood of His cross; we also have peace of heart and conscience because sin is expiated through His sacrifice. We also have healing, in the sense of forgiveness and regeneration. Sin is often set forth in the form of sickness. This same prophet (Isaiah) says of Israel, in connection with their sins: "The whole head is sick, and the whole heart faint. From the sole of the foot even

CHRIST IN ISAIAH FIFTY-THREE

unto the head there is no soundness in it; but wounds and bruises and putrifying sores." So we are healed. But this healing means more than that —and what healing is not of Him?—for it goes on to that day when all physical and spiritual disease and blemish shall be eternally healed in our conformity to His own image and body of glory (Phil. 3:20, 21).

The intensity of our Lord's sufferings is indicated in these words: "wounded"—literally, "pierced through" or "wounded to death;" "bruised"—literally, "crushed," by the heavy burden of our sins, which He took unto Himself, and which were visited by the wrath of God.

We wish to note also the pronouns in this verse. There is a sharp and distinct antithesis here: *we, our, us,* on one side; *He, His, Him,* on the other.

"We" indicates many; "He" indicates One. There is no question as to who the "we" are, for He is the propitiation not for our sins only, but also for the sins of the whole world; neither is there any question as to who "He" is, for in all heaven, earth, and hell there is only One, our great God and Savior, Jesus Christ. *We* transgressed, *He* was wounded for our transgressions; *we* lived in iniquity, *He* bore the stroke for our iniquity; *we* sinned, *He* died under sin's wage and due.

The responsibility for His death is ours. In Zech. 12:10 we read these prophetic words: "They shall look upon Me Whom they have pierced." Sinner, saint—all—shall we look now? Shall we see Him pierced for us? Wounds speak more forcibly than words. When the crippled boys came home from the World War, their condition spoke more loudly than the tongue of the orator. Never were wounds so eloquent as those suffered by our Lord. His wounds tell us about sin—oh, if you would know what sin really is—the crushing, overwhelming weight of sin, you must wend your way to Calvary's cross. His wounds tell us about love—if you want to know the limits of love, look to the wounds of Calvary.

Some one has pled with sinners to look to Him Who is pierced, somewhat as follows:

Look at those hands pierced with nails, and then say, "My Lord, my Lord, why are Thy hands so pierced?" Then look at your own hands for the answer. Your hands wrought out your own will. Your hands are guilty hands. Your hands should have been pierced. Then hear the Lord plead for thee: "O Father, that sinner's hands are stained with guilt; they have wrought his own will; but these hands of mine have always done Thy will; from Bethlehem they have wrought only that which brought Thy smile. Father, take these guiltless hands of Mine, and nail them to the Cross, and when the nails have pierced My hands, then let this sinner's guilty hands go free."

Look at those feet pierced with nails, and then say, "My Lord, my Lord, why are Thy feet so pierced?" Then look at your own feet for the answer. Your feet have led you far astray. Your feet have travelled your own way. Your feet should have been pierced. Then hear the Lord plead for thee: "O Father, the feet of this sinner have travelled the path of sin, and they have led him down the road to hell, but My feet have always been found in the path of right, and have always led me swiftly to do Thy will. Father, take these feet of Mine, and nail them to the Cross, and when the nails have pierced My feet, let the feet of this sinner tread the path of life."

Look through the wound in that riven side to see the heart pierced with a spear, and then say, "My Lord, my Lord, tell me why Thy heart is pierced and broken." Then look at your own heart for the answer. Your heart has been deceitful and desperately wicked. Your heart should have been pierced and broken. Then hear the Lord plead for thee: "O Father, that sinner's heart has been full of evil; the stains of sin and guilt are upon it; demons have dwelt there; but, Father, My heart has been pure and stainless; it has been in sweet harmony with Thy will from first to last; never a thought was harbored there in which Thou couldst not delight; Father, take this guiltless heart of mine, and let the weight of a world's sin rest upon it—the crushing weight of a world's guilt—crush it, bruise it, break it, and when I have suffered to the full, and am broken under the weary load, then fill the sinner's heart with heaven's own joy; pour in the power of an endless life; make that heart a garden of Eden, in which are planted the seeds of God's life. From my pierced heart may there come the blood and the water that shall wash that guilty heart of his, and make him clean."

Sinner, look, believing, and be saved. Saint, look too, and from His presence go forth to tell to lost men everywhere that "He was wounded for our transgressions." Look, that the soul may be fed, and the desires purified.

In conclusion we quote from Dr. I. M. Haldeman, who, in speaking of the Civil War, writes: "One day when the sound of the cannon came on the wind I was halted with others on the side of the road that a convoy of the wounded might pass. They were loaded into great carts and wagons impressed from neighboring farms. And these wounded! They were young men, the flower and freshness of the land; and when I saw the bandaged heads and arms still reddened with their blood my heart melted within me, and the tears leaped to my eyes. I saw in these men the radiance of that self-sacrifice, that high and lofty concept which counts a flag to be worth more than any single life; and these wounds and blood stains were to me the stigmata of unfaltering faith and abiding glory, the decorations and brevet of honor, of high attainment and of splendor, nor rank, nor pomp, nor wealth, nor crown of prince could give.

"But what were these stigmata, these seals of honor and devotion on the part of those who had breasted death that a nation might be saved, what were these compared to the stigmata of Him Who died for you and me, good friend, that we might live and be with Him in after days, the sons of God forever?

"He is coming back with the marks of the nails and the spear wound He received for you and me. And I shall see Him, see Him by the right of the purchase price paid in the blood of those very wounds. I shall take His hand; how can I endure the wonder, the glory, and the anguish even of the joy and the reality of it? I shall put my fingers into the marks of the nails in His right hand. I shall do it as Thomas did it, and yet not as Thomas did. I shall not do it to prove Him, to verify Him, but to thank Him; and I shall say, 'It was for me.' I shall put my hand into His side where the spear point was sheathed in His breast, and where water and blood came forth from His broken heart, and I shall say, 'It was for me;' and I shall fall down and kiss the nail-marks in His feet and every full running tear of joy and praise shall say, 'These were for me'."

"By Thy sweat, bloody and clotted! Thy soul in
    agony,
Thy head crowned with thorns, bruised with staves,
Thine eyes a fountain of tears,
Thine ears full of insults,
Thy mouth moistened with vinegar and gall,
Thy face stained with spitting,
Thy neck bowed down with the burden of the
    Cross,
Thy back ploughed with the welts and wounds of
    the scourge,
Thy pierced hands and feet,
Thy strong cry, Eli, Eli,
Thy heart pierced with the spear,
The water and blood thence flowing,
Thy body broken, Thy blood poured out—
Lord, forgive the iniquity of Thy servant
And cover all his sin."

His Moral Obligation

> *"All we like sheep have gone astray; we have turned every one to his own way; and the Lord hath laid on Him the iniquity of us all"* (Isaiah 53:6).

ISAIAH'S prophecy has to do with the vision "which he saw concerning Judah and Jerusalem" (1:1). He was a Hebrew prophet speaking to the Hebrews concerning their own nation. In Isaiah 53:6 the nation of Israel is pictured as a scattered flock, all "going astray" from the pasture and the protection of their Shepherd. Many believe that this fifty-third chapter is the confession which Israel will make at the time of Christ's second coming. We know, however, that the work of the Messiah is no more limited to them than the work of Christ is limited to Paul when he says, "The Son of God...loved me, and gave Himself for me." John declares that He is the propitiation "for the sins of the whole world." "God so loved the *world* that He gave His only begotten Son." Not only the sufferings of the Savior, but the sins of the people admit of universal application, so that we have in this sixth verse a picture of the whole human race.

This verse begins and ends with an "all." It includes *all* of us in sin. It includes *all* of us in the redemption which Christ provides.

All Are Sinners

"All we like sheep have *gone astray.*" The whole human race has gone away from God. This is a clear presentation of the wretchedness of our natural condition. Men are wholly estranged from God. They suffer the loss of safety and happiness. The Hebrew word which is here translated "gone astray" is full of suggestion. It means to vacillate; i. e., to reel, or stagger, or stray; and suggests deception, delusion, excitement, agitation, seduction. It gives us the picture of a wanderer, moving about without any fixed destination. The wanderer is lost. He is panting, not because of weariness, but because of agitation. It is the picture of a soul astray from God. He is restless and ill at ease. "There is no peace, saith my God, to the wicked." The thought of deception is in this word—the idea that the sinner has been seduced into his present straying and lost condition, precisely as we read in the story of the Fall as recorded in Genesis 3, where man is deceived and seduced by Satan. How perfectly true are all these figures to describe the sinner as we know him, as we have known ourselves! "The Devil goeth about as a roaring lion seeking whom he may devour," and sinners are absolutely helpless against him. They are wandering over the dark mountains of sin, relying on their own strength and guidance, and will eventually come to grief. Over them are the black storm clouds of God's wrath against sin, ready to break in judgment, and they are without the Shepherd's care and protection. On slippery paths they approach the precipice of death over which they will soon plunge, if they are not saved.

> "Like sheep we went astray
> And broke the fold of God;
> Each wand'ring in a different way,
> But all the downward road."

"All we *like sheep* have gone astray." It seems natural for a sheep to go astray. This is a sad picture of the human heart. Man will stray away from God although he has every reason to stay with Him. The Shepherd is good, the pasture is ample, the care is wise and tender, the protection is sure, and yet man

41

will stray away from Him. Sheep may not be to blame for wandering; they know no better; but in men, who have reasoning power, conscience, and Scripture, wandering means sin.

A sheep goes astray differently from any other animal. A horse, a dog, a cat or any other domestic animal will return to its old home, if given liberty to do so, but when a sheep wanders away it pursues its wandering, never returning of its own accord. If a wandering sheep ever returns, it is because the shepherd brings it back. It is true that "the ox knoweth his owner, and the ass his master's crib," but the sheep does not know and seems not to consider. Man who has gone away from God needs a Savior, and apart from that Savior man never has returned, and never will return. Education, legislation, reformation will never bring him back.

A sheep goes astray in ignorance. No matter where the shepherd leads, there is a path that to the sheep seems better, and it makes its way along that path, not knowing that in all probability it will end in a precipice and death. So with man. "There is a way that seemeth right unto a man, but the end thereof are the ways of death" (Prov. 14:12).

A sheep in going astray will wander from one place to another, from one patch of grass to another, but does not know the peace and fulness that come from lying down "in green pastures." So the sinner, with reprobate mind and blind eye, seeks contentment, first in this direction and then in that, and never finds it. The sinner is always empty and dissatisfied. The picture of every sinner was drawn, in a measure at least, by Byron, when, in giving his own experience, he wrote that he

"Drank every cup of joy,
Heard every trump of fame,
Drank early, deeply drank,
Drank draughts which common millions might have
    quenched,

Then died of thirst, because there was no more to
   drink."

A sheep gone astray is helpless. He is the prey
of evil. He has no David to deliver him from the
lion and the bear. The sinner is helpless against the
attacks of Satan.

Sheep imitate one another. As Pastor E. L. James
says, "Adam, the old bell-wether, went out over the
fence long ago, and every last son of Adam has gone
over ever since." Human nature still follows the
bell-wether. In this connection it would be well for
the sinner to think of the power of his example upon
his fellowman. We cannot help influencing one another. The sinner's influence is not for Christ nor
for holiness. Many a soul has gone out into the
dark, dismal night of separation from God because
one stray sheep has influenced another.

"All we like sheep have gone astray." There is a
universality in sin here. The whole human race has
gone astray, in Adam potentially, in life actually.
All have sinned, without exception. All have forsak-
en and disregarded and grieved God. There is none
righteous, no, not one. They are all gone out of
the way. There is none that doeth good, no, not one.
Destruction and misery are in their ways. The way
of peace have they not known. Read Romans 3 if
you would know the universality and totality of sin.

All Are Self-Willed

All sinners are alike. Many a sinner will not agree
to this statement. The refined sinner will look at the
coarse sinner and declare that he is altogether dif-
ferent. The world will not agree to this statement.
The world will open its arms and take to its bosom
the cultured sinner, but will cast out the rough and
the rude and the ignorant. The world thinks there
is a difference between sinners. Too many times the
church will not agree with this statement, for it
makes a difference between the moneyed and the

moneyless sinner. We are sure, however, that to God all sinners are alike. "There is no difference; for all have sinned and come short of the glory of God."

Notice that we have not said that all *sins*, but that all *sinners* are alike. Sins may differ in kind and in number, but every sinner is like every other sinner in the sense of the words of our text: "We have turned every one to his own way." Every sinner is like every other sinner in that he takes his own way and does his own will instead of God's. Pride, vanity, covetousness, murder, adultery, and all other sins come from the same source. It makes no difference to sinners what God says, they persist in their sins. The question men need to answer is not, "How reputable am I?" but "Whose will am I doing?" While there is unity in sin, there is diversity in its manifestation. All men have sinful natures, but God does not hate them for that. Man is not accountable for his sinful nature, but he is for his sinful acts. You did not have to tell an untruth. You did not have to blaspheme. You sinned, but you did not have to sin. "No one can charge the guilt of his own sin on any one else. On whom, or on what, will you cast the blame? On influences? But it was for you to resist and not to yield. On temptation? But temptations cannot force. There is no forcing of the will either to right or to wrong. An action forced on a man irrespective of his will is chargeable to the one who forced him." *Will cannot be forced.* Every sin is an act of will. "We have turned every one (literally, each man) to his own way." This is the very opposite of the way of God. We have all gone in the path which we chose. We have not entered into the thoughts of God, nor endeavored to follow His ways, but we have gone on the broad way of our own. "To will to do God's will is man's highest privilege, his most godlike prerogative." But ever since man yielded to the temptation of Satan, the mind of the flesh has been "enmity against God" (Rom. 8:7).

44

We might state this truth in another way by saying that sin is selfishness (*selfness* might be better) which ends in suicide, for sin in its finality is suicide. Man desires to have his own way even though it leads to disease, disaster, death. Every sin can be traced back to selfishness as the cause.

Sin is an awful truth, affirmed in Scripture and universally acknowledged by individuals. Its horrors no power can paint. No fiction can color its terrible reality. Dean Law writes: "It is man's ruin...It made the heart a nest of unclean birds; a spring of impure streams; a whirlpool of tumultuous passions; a hot-bed of ungodly lusts; a den of God-defying schemes. It is the malady—the misery—the shame of our whole race. It is the spring of every tear. Each sigh, which rends the breast; each frown, which ploughs the brow; each pain, which racks the limbs, is cradled in its arms. It is the mother of that mighty monster, death. It digs each grave in every grave-yard. Its terrible destructions die not in the grave. There is a region where its full-blown torments reign. It built the prison house of hell. It kindled quenchless flames. It forged the chains which bind lost sinners to their burning beds. It sharpened the undying sting of an upbraiding conscience. It bars the hopeless where weeping never ceases, and wailing is never stilled; where teeth forever gnash, and all is woe which knows no respite and no end."

Sin is against God. The sinner raises his clenched and rebel hand against God's will. He tramples on the statute book of heaven. He strives to lay God's honor in the dust.

All Can Be Saved

It is because men are wholly estranged from God that the death of Jesus Christ was necessary. God's moral law is inflexible and His own righteousness and justice absolute. This binds the Ruler of the universe to render to every one his due. The penalty incurred by transgression must be inflicted. If the penalty might be set aside in one instance, it might be in all, and then God's government would be at an end, with nothing but moral ruin and wreckage for the universe. The moral obligation that rested upon God was to see that His righteousness was upheld in all of the proceedings of His government. God could not justify the sinner at the expense of His own righteousness. The requisite satisfaction must be made to God's law and justice.

This moral obligation God discharged, and the manner in which it was done is set forth in the text of this message: "The Lord hath laid on Him the iniquity of us all." Thus the problem that no finite intelligence or created wisdom could solve was accomplished by Divine wisdom. God had love for man, but only hatred for man's sins. God had mercy for His creatures, but no mercy for their transgressions. The justice of God was an obstacle to the mercy of God. Justice cried, "Smite!" while Mercy pled, "Save." The wanderings of earth are the care of heaven, and so by an appointment in heaven the sin of all was laid upon Him Who came as the Servant of Jehovah.

"The Lord hath laid on Him the *iniquity* of us all." "Iniquity" denotes not only transgression, but its guilt and punishment also. The thought is expressed in II Cor. 5:21: "He who knew no sin was made to be sin." The word translated "of us all" is the very word with which this verse begins: "All we." As "all we" are included in sin and guilt, so also are *we all* included in the provision of God's redeeming grace. Alexander rightly states that the words "laid upon Him" are too weak, because they "suggest the idea of a mild and inoffensive gesture, whereas that conveyed by the Hebrew word is necessarily a violent one, viz., that of causing to strike or fall." Benjamin Wills Newton states that here our iniquity is spoken of as "coming upon Him like a destroying foe and overwhelming Him with the wrath that it brought with it." Alexander also states that "If vicarious suffering can be described in words, it is so described in these two verses" (Isaiah 53:5, 6). J. F. B. notes: "The innocent was punished as if guilty, that the guilty might be rewarded as if innocent. This verse could be said of no mere martyr."

It was Jehovah who caused all of our iniquity to light, or strike, upon Him. He it was Who placed this awful burden upon Him. What the law could not do, God has accomplished. He has condemned sin without destroying the sinner, through laying the great burden on One, Who, in bearing it, has made it vanish away forever!

Among men there are those who say that the substitution of the innocent for the guilty is unjust. In answer we say that such a substitution is admissible when wrought out according to the wisdom and the will of our holy and righteous God. It is altogether unreasonable to complain of any injustice here, since Jesus Christ Himself came and volunteered to take the sinner's place, in order to remove those obstacles which stood in the way of the sinner's salvation. As Clemance says: "No doubt it would be unjust that the innocent should suffer for the guilty without reason. But if the suffering be voluntarily incurred, and the sufferer is fully satisfied with the reason for it, and the result of it, the charge of injustice can no longer show any even apparent ground." These objectors are mere reasoners without the Book, which states that Christ suffered, "the Just for the unjust"; that "Christ died for our sins."

We need to remember that our salvation through the vicarious sufferings and death of Christ had its origin in the love of God. "God so loved the world that He gave His only begotten Son"—gave Him up into the hands of justice to die in our stead. "Herein is love, not that we loved God, but that He loved us, and sent His Son to be the propitiation for our sins" (I John 4:10). "God commendeth His love toward us, in that, while we were yet sinners, Christ died for us" (Romans 5:8). It is this love of God for the lost that has created a dispensation of grace, in which God might Himself be just, even while justifying the sinner "that hath faith in Jesus" (Rom. 3:26, R. V.).

Who was sufficient for this substitutionary work? No mere man could be the substitute, for all men are sinful, and He Who was to remove sin must not Himself be liable to it. He Who was to be the Substitute for the guilty must Himself be innocent. He Who was to suffer in the stead of the disobedient must Himself be obedient in all things. Then again, the sufferings and death of one man could not possess the merit to answer the demands of the law against a world of men. Neither could any person of the Godhead perform the work of redemption. The Deity could not die. This substitute, in order to suffer for sin, must be human. More than that, He must have infinite merit. Nothing that is not Divine is infinite. This difficulty can be overcome only by the constitution of a Person in whom these two natures are united. So a Babe was born to a virgin, and was called Emmanuel—God with us! God in incarnation brought human nature into such intimate union with Himself that the sufferings and death of that nature were the sufferings and death of the person of the Son of God. To remove the curse pronounced in the law of God for disobedience, He had to undergo the punishment which in the Word is declared to be the curse of God. That punishment is hanging on a tree (Deut. 21:24). "Christ hath redeemed us from the curse of the law, being made a curse for us: for it is written, cursed is every one that hangeth on a tree: That the blessing of Abraham might come on the Gentiles through Jesus Christ" (Gal. 3:13, 14). That Abrahamic blessing is justification by faith. Having accepted the curse, He liberated us from it.

"He suffered in our stead, He saved His people thus;
The curse that fell upon His head was due by right
    to us.
The storm that bowed His blessed head is hushed
    forever now,
And rest Divine is mine instead, while glory crowns
    His brow."

There is no salvation through a denial of sin and
its punishment, but when we believe "the record that
God gave of His Son" (I John 5:10), grace is manifested, and the guilty are saved. Salvation becomes
effective only through faith. The universal testimony
of the New Testament is "Believe on the Lord Jesus
Christ and thou shalt be saved" (Acts 16:31). Calvary meets the sinner's need and satisfies the Savior's heart.

We close with this testimony: "I am free from
guilt the moment I believe, and now I love and learn
to do right, not from fear that after all I should not
be saved, but from love, because I *am* saved! Christ's
substitutionary sacrifice on the cross is to me the
Lamp of Life. I have but to believe Jesus, and plead
His death in the room of mine, and when once I
take that position, there is not an angel in heaven
comes nearer to God than I can, not one approaches
Him with more acceptance, not one receives sweeter
smiles than I! Oh, how this Cross relieves me! How
it sweetens life! How bright it makes my hopes!
How charmed it makes life's duties! All was a burden till I understood the Cross!"

Can we all say, from the heart, what the poet has
written?

"But drops of grief can ne'er repay
    The debt of love I owe;
Here, Lord, I give myself to Thee,
    'Tis all that I can do."

Chapter VI

His Meritorious Death

*"He was oppressed, and He was afflicted, yet
He opened not His mouth: He is brought as a
lamb to the slaughter, and as a sheep before her
shearers is dumb, so He openeth not His
mouth" (Isaiah 53:7).*

IT WAS from these very words that Philip
preached the gospel which proved to be the power of God unto salvation to the Ethiopean
eunuch. "Then Philip opened his mouth, and began at the same Scripture, and preached unto him
Jesus." He preached that Jesus was led as a lamb to
the slaughter, and that His life was taken from the
earth (Acts 8:32-35). The eunuch believed, confessed
Christ with his mouth, confessed Him in baptism, and
went on his way rejoicing. Philip began at the central
point of the world's history—the Cross of Calvary.
That is the point to which the eyes of the universe are
turned. The Devil and his demons are looking at the
Cross. If they could blot out Calvary they would gain
a world. The holy angels are looking at the Cross,
and as souls, redeemed by its power, come home
to the glory of Jehovah's presence, they sing: "Worthy is the Lamb that was slain." Saints of all ages
are looking at the Cross, and each happy, ransomed
soul is saying, "God forbid that I should glory save in
the Cross of our Lord Jesus Christ." God is looking
at the Cross. His eyes are never off it. He rules the
course of the world and deals with human hearts in
the light of it. When God begins the work of the salvation of a human soul, He always begins, like Philip,

at "the same Scripture"—He begins with the Lamb slain. And now, in the study of this Scripture we, too, shall look at His Cross.

> "Upon the Cross of Jesus,
>   Mine eyes at times can see
> The very dying form of One,
>   Who suffered there for me;
> And from my smitten heart with tears,
>   Two wonders I confess,
> The wonders of His glorious love,
>   And my unworthiness."

His Sacrifice

We suppose that every reference to the Lamb of God in the New Testament springs from this verse in Isaiah, for undoubtedly the prophet had in mind the lamb that was being continually sacrificed in the offerings of Israel, including the Passover.

The Old Testament sacrifices were instituted by God as types of Christ. No other satisfactory reason can be advanced for the custom of offering sacrifice. They all point to the great sacrifice of the Redeemer. This thought did not originate with man. In the garden in Eden before the fall there was no sacrifice, for there was no sin to confess and no justice to be satisfied. The first record in Scripture of an animal sacrifice by man is in Genesis 4:4, where Abel brought a firstling of his flock as an offering to Jehovah. This offering Abel brought to God, not because of some law written in his natural heart, but because of "faith" (Hebrews 11:4), which indicates that it was in obedience to a command of God. Most certainly no human invention can please God. And surely these sacrifices could only prefigure some sufficient sacrifice. They were for the purpose of instruction. They all pointed off to a day when there should be a sacrifice eternally efficacious, as exhibited in our Lord and Savior, Jesus Christ. These animal sacrifices were only

51

shadows, and could "never take away sins," and could never "make the comers thereunto perfect" (Heb. 10:1, 11). They testified to the sins of men, but could only provide a typical salvation. Their repetition year in and year out evidenced their insufficiency. Had sin been expiated by them, the fire would not have been kept continually burning, fed perpetually with the carcasses of beasts. The continual reiteration of sacrifices loudly proclaimed the fact that the guilt of sin was not wiped out, the justice and holiness of God were not satisfied. Again, propitiation through the blood of a beast would not be consistent with the honor and majesty of God, against whom man sins. Our holy God on the holy mount gave His holy law, and amid the thunders and lightnings and earthquake solemnly declared a curse against the transgressor. Was that law so light a thing that the death of a few poor beasts, irrational and innocent creatures who had never broken that law, could provide proper compensation for the terrible curse against the offender? Is that the extent of God's hatred against sin? Could the blood of a beast expiate the foul sin of man? Reason, and conscience, too, cry out "No!" and that cry is but the echo of the Word of God which states that "It is not possible that the blood of bulls and goats should take away sin" (Heb. 10:4).

We know that God's sacrifice must be consistent with God's being. Furthermore, man himself would not be a sufficient sacrifice to meet the holy and righteous demands of God, for man is sinful and defiled. The least blemish in a typical lamb rendered it unfit for the altar. Then, too, sin is infinite, for every sin is against the Infinite God, a fact which makes it an infinite offense, that can never find its equivalent in a finite sacrifice. Some one has written: "If every hair of our head were a soul, and every soul a sacrifice, all would be too poor an amend for that glorious God wronged by us, though it had been but by one act of rebellion." Yea, though all men in the world were

sacrificed together, that sacrifice would not be sufficient to provide their own redemption. They must still
be eternally overwhelmed by the wrath of God.

There is such an inconceivable distance between the
Creator and His Creatures that their salvation can be
procured only by God Incarnate—none other than
Jesus Christ Himself. He answers to these types. He
literally fulfilled them. He was used in such a manner
as the figures of Him were. On Him Jehovah laid the
"iniquity of us all." The demerit of sin and the se-
verity of Divine justice, as well as Divine love, were
manifested at the Cross. The whole sacrificial ritual
of Israel was completed in Him when He cried, "It
is finished." He alone was fit to be this sacrifice fulfilling all other sacrifices, for He had a human body
"prepared," and He was "equal with God" (Heb. 10:5;
Phil. 2:6). Charnock says: "He could treat with God,
as partaking of His glory, and be a sacrifice for man,
as partaking of the infirmities of his nature; He had
a body to bear the stroke due to a victim, and a Divine nature to sustain Him under it; He had a human
nature to offer as a sacrifice, and a Divine nature
to render it valuable and infinitely meritorious; being
God and man, He wanted not a fitness to accomplish
so great an undertaking. If He had not been man, He
could not have been a sacrifice; and if He had not
been God, He could not have been a remedy." We are
shut up to Jesus Christ as a Savior. "'Neither is there
salvation in any other: for there is none other name
under heaven given among men whereby we must be
saved" (Acts 4:12). We would take our stand with
John the Baptist and plead with men: "Behold the
Lamb of God that taketh away the sin of the world!"

His Submission

In the great Shepherd discourse in John 10 our
Lord said: "I lay down My life for the sheep . . .
Therefore doth My Father love Me, because I lay
down My life, that I might take it again. No man

53

taketh it from Me, but I lay it down of Myself. I have the power to lay it down, and I have the power to take it again" (verses 15-18). It is true that men with wicked hands took Him and crucified Him. It is true that Jehovah laid on Him the iniquity of us all. It is also true that He undertook suffering, shame, sorrow, sacrifice, voluntarily. He "gave Himself." The Father gave Him; He offered Himself (Eph. 5: 2). Christ is one with God the Father, and there is but one and the same will in both. The decree of redemption was the decree of the Godhead. What Christ decreed as God, He executed as man. What He willed from eternity, He began in time to will as man. He is called again and again in the Word, "the Sent One." That does not mean that He was thrust out of heaven, and forced to come to earth and to the Cross. It does not mean that He was over-persuaded. It does not mean merely that He came in obedience. It means that the inclination to come was His own. It was His feet that were shod with love that carried Him all the way from glory to Calvary. He was the Actor in all the work of redemption, not merely one upon whom some action was taken. The Incarnation was His own act. In John 1:14 (R. V.) which reads: "The Word became flesh," the word "became" is one, not of passivity, but of activity. By His own will and power He became flesh. Verify this by Heb. 2:14: "For as much then as the children are partakers of flesh and blood, He also Himself likewise took part of the *same*." We read in II Cor. 8:9 that "Though He was rich, yet for your sakes, He became poor," but He was not made poor by force. He was not emptied of His glory by another: He emptied Himself (Phil. 2:7, R. V.). He "made Himself of no reputation." He "took upon Him the form of a servant." He "humbled Himself." This was not imposed upon Him by constraint. He was not debased by others. All was voluntary, including His death. He "hath given Himself for us, an offering, and a sacrifice to God" (Eph.

5:2). His voluntary sacrifice is set forth in the typical lamb, the mildest of creatures, resisting neither the shearer nor the butcher. Love led Him to die an ignominious death, under the legal curse of God, that He might deliver us from a deserved hell, and receive us into an undeserved heaven. He could have delivered Himself. When the motley crowd with swords and staves came to take Him, His word and the majesty of His presence sent them prostrate to the ground. He could have walked away from them. He was led as a lamb to the slaughter only because He yielded Himself into their hands—the Creator in the hands of His creatures! *Had He resisted, He would have conquered.* He could have delivered Himself from the hands of men, but He did not; therefore His death was voluntary.

This is what made His sacrificial death one of merit. Had Christ not willingly offered Himself, justice would have been wronged instead of satisfied. It certainly would not be just to punish one who was not guilty, against His will. Had Christ died by constraint, justice might have been satisfied in one way, but it surely would have been tremendously injured in another way. The will of Christ could not have saved us without His suffering and death; the suffering and death of Christ could not have saved us without His will. But

"As a sheep by the shearer is meekly led,
He endureth it for us, and no word He said,
　　Bearing His Cross.
Though He knew what it meant, yet He turned not his back,
But He patiently trod all the weary track,
　　Bearing His Cross.
They had never been able to lead Him thus,
If He had not been willing to die for us,
　　Bearing His Cross."

This is the secret of these words: "He was oppressed, and He was afflicted, yet He opened not His mouth." He suffered voluntarily. There are a number of renderings given to these words which set forth His sufferings. "He was ill-treated whilst He bowed Himself." "He was used violently, though He humbled Himself." David Baron states that the rendering that, in his judgment, comes nearer the true sense of the original is: "It was exacted, and He was made answerable, and He opened not His mouth"; or the following paraphrase: "He was rigorously demanded to pay the debt, and He submitted Himself, and did not open His mouth." There is no question concerning the truth set forth here by Isaiah. Jesus Christ bowed Himself under the burden of sin, and in spite of being used violently, He suffered in lamblike meekness the stroke of God's justice against it. "He loved me, and gave Himself for me."

His Silence

Twice in this verse it is stated that our Lord opened not His mouth. In order to understand the closed mouth of the Savior it is necessary to look at the closed mouth of the sinner. In Romans 3:19 we read: "Now we know that what things soever the law saith, it saith to them that are under the law: that every mouth may be stopped, and all the world may become guilty before God." The law never saved; it only proved those who were under the law to be sinners. At Sinai, when God gave the law, Israel opened her mouth, and said, "All that the Lord hath spoken we will do" (Exodus 19:8). Almost before the echo of their voices died away the golden calf was set up, the law was broken, and they were speechless in their unrighteousness. This will be the effect upon every sinner when he honestly faces the holy law of God, especially under the spiritual application made by our Lord, as, for example, when He stated: "Ye have heard that it was said by them of old time, Thou shalt not commit adultery: But I say unto you, That whosoever looketh on a woman to lust after her hath committed adultery with her already in his heart" (Matt. 5:27-28). Go down the line of all the commandments with this spiritual application, and your mouth will be stopped. No one will be able to claim the perfect righteousness which pleases God. Sin closes the mouth.

Now think of the closed mouth of the Savior. The only One Who ever did live in obdience to the law, the only One Who ever did have a right to open His mouth, opened it not.

"And the high priest arose, and said unto Him, Answerest Thou nothing? what is it which these witness against Thee? But Jesus held His peace."

"And when He was accused of the chief priests and elders, He answered nothing."

"Then said Pilate unto Him, Hearest Thou not how many things they witness against Thee? And He answered him never a word; insomuch that the governor marvelled greatly" (Matt. 26:62, 63; 27:12-14).

He stood in the presence of His accusers—a silent Christ. He could have opened His mouth, for He was sinless. He could have opened His mouth in His own defense. He could have opened His mouth to call twelve legions of angels, but He was dumb with silence. Why was it He opened not His mouth? Because He came to do the will of His Father. Why was it He opened not His mouth? Because He came to redeem lost men. Why was it He opened not His mouth? Because He loved you—and me.

He could have opened His mouth. You cannot. Your mouth is stopped. You are a sinner.

He could have opened His mouth to save Himself; to save us He opened it not.

> "Why was He silent, when a word
>   Would slay His accusers all?
> Why does He meekly bear their taunts,
>   When angels wait His call?

'He was made sin'; my sin He bore
   Upon the accursed tree;
And sin hath no defense to make—
   His silence was for me."

We close with a warning based on the parable of the man without the wedding garment, recorded in Matthew 22:1-13. According to Oriental custom each guest at a wedding had to wear a garment which was provided by the father of the groom. Just as the father supplied the wedding garment, so God supplies us with a robe of righteousness, when we become believers on His Son. Are you robed? Make sure of this.

When the king, whose son was to be married, came suddenly among the wedding guests, he saw one without the wedding garment, and caused him to be thrust out into the night and into the darkness. He was separated from the rest of the guests. He did not see the son.

There is judgment in this parable—we want you to see it. That man represents the unaved one who is cast out. The king did not condemn that man unheard. He went to the man, "And he saith unto him, 'Friend, how camest thou in hither not having a wedding garment? *And he was speechless.*" This is the closed mouth in the judgment.

Christ died for you, sinner. God graciously invites you to believe on Him, and to take your place among the company of the redeemed. When you do this, Christ will be made unto you righteousness. Your mouth is closed because of sin. His mouth was closed because He was sin's substitute. Open your mouth now and confess Him as Savior, "For with the mouth confession is made unto salvation." So you shall not stand speechless before God in judgment.

Because Jesus Christ chose to pay the price of our redemption, He did not interfere in His own behalf. The only time He did speak, when He was on trial, was to guide the trial into right channels. He gave an affirmative answer when the high priest demanded (contrary to Jewish law): "I adjure Thee, by the living God, that Thou tell us whether Thou be the Christ, the Son of God." He would stand before the earthly tribunal as the Son of God and the King of glory. He made no effort to vindicate Himself from false accusers. The future would do that. The resurrection would do that. But remember that Jesus Christ was not always silent. His lips overflowed with grace. And the most gracious words that He ever spoke were these: "Thy sins are forgiven. Thy faith hath saved thee" (Luke 7:48-50). Sinner, when He speaks peace to your soul, you will join with others in saying: "Never man spake like this Man!"

Chapter VII

His Mysterious Experience

> "He was taken from prison and from judg-
> ment: and who shall declare His generation?
> for He was cut off out of the land of the liv-
> ing: for the transgression of my people was
> He stricken. And He made His grave with
> the wicked and with the rich in His death;
> because He had done no violence, neither was
> any deceit in His mouth" (Isaiah 53:8, 9).

HE death of Christ has been called the "mystery of mysteries." This is because of the
Personality involved in suffering and death.
The transcendent mystery and glory of the
cross was that God Himself was on it. In its last,
and awful, and blessed meaning, the giving of the
Only Begotten Son was God's giving of Himself for
the sins of the world. "God was in Christ, reconcil-
ing the world unto Himself" (II Cor. 5:19). The
agony that pierced the soul of the Crucified, in some
unimaginable way pierced the very heart of God.
No wonder that the angels desire to look into this
transcendent mystery of love. "Oh, the depth of the
riches both of the wisdom and knowledge of God!
how unsearchable are His judgments, and His ways
past finding out!" (Romans 11:33).

There is in the cross a mystery so deep that even
angels cannot sound it. The philosophic contemplation of all the ages will never exhaust it. Yet
there is in the Gospel a simplicity which even a child
can apprehend. It is this: *Christ died for us.* This
is the truth set forth in the verses of this present
study.

His Trial

There is, perhaps, no verse in this great prophetic chapter (Isaiah 53) that has been so variously rendered by Bible students and translators as the eighth verse. The first words of this verse are, in the Authorized Version: "He was taken from prison and from judgment"; and in the Revised Version: "By oppression and judgment was He taken away." Alexander renders it, "From distress and from judgment He was taken"; probably meaning that He was released from His sufferings by death. Lowth writes it, "He was taken away (i. e., cut off) by oppression and by a judicial sentence." "After condemnation and judgment He was accepted," says Horsley. "Hurried was He from prison and judgment"—thus Jennings. The Septuagint translates, "In His humiliation His judgment (legal trial) was taken away," and this is sanctioned by the inspired writer of Acts. Philip, in quoting this passage to the man of Ethiopia, declares: "In His humiliation His judgment was taken away" (Acts 8:33). Henderson makes it, "Without restraint and without a sentence He was taken away." All of the shades of thought in these various translations are true. He was taken out of the midst of sufferings by death, and in this way was delivered from them. He was put to death without opposition from any quarter, and in defiance of justice. He exercised no manner of restraint over His persecutors. He was executed without proper trial or sentence. His death was in violation of every principle of justice. His judgment was unjust. He was judicially murdered.

The word translated "judgment" undoubtedly refers to the judicial proceedings in which He was put on trial, accused, and convicted as worthy of death. The word translated "taken" has in it the idea of being hurried away. Clemance says, "According to usage, the word implies a forcible snatching off." Certainly we have here the thought of the "violence

61

which cloaked itself under the formalities of a legal process," and the illegal haste with which the unjust proceedings were carried on.

The trial of our Lord is the most famous trial in the history of criminal law, but more than that, it is, as some one has said, "the greatest monstrosity in the annals of legal history." He was treated as one so mean that a fair trial was denied Him. The hostile oppression sought false witnesses against Him, but not a single witness was heard in His behalf.

Our Lord went through two trials: one, the Jewish, or ecclesiastical trial; the other, the Roman, or civil trial. He was arrested possibly about midnight, and taken before Annas for a preliminary hearing sometime after one o'clock. From the home of Annas He was sent to Caiaphas, the high priest, and to the Sanhedrin, ·where He was tried and condemned for *blasphemy* before six o'clock in the morning. Then He was hurried to Pilate very early in the morning; from whose presence He was hurried to be scourged and crucified, under the charge of *sedition*—not the charge on which He was condemned by the Jewish council. The Roman trial was necessary because of the subjection of Israel to Rome. The Jewish council, or Sanhedrin, had authority to try capital cases according to their own law, but, in case of a conviction, the Roman governor was required to review the case and confirm or reverse the decision. So the Jews had to take Jesus before Pilate, the Roman governor, to have their sentence of death ratified.

The irregularities and illegalities in the trial of our Lord are astounding. In fact, He was tried, condemned, and sentenced to death by the Jewish council before He ever came to trial. (Read John 11: 46-57 and Matt. 6:3-5 and Luke 22:1-3). This was in direct violation of the Jewish law—in fact, a violation of every decent law. We suggest a few of the injustices of His trial as indicated by Dr. Branch in his booklet, "The Trial of Jesus." He was arrested at night, and tried at night, both in direct violation of the Jewish law. Annas and Caiaphas sat alone in each case, in direct violation of the Jewish law, which declared that "judges" should try a case (Deut. 19:16-19). Caiaphas sought to make Jesus incriminate Himself, in direct violation of the Jewish law. The trial was opened with no previously prepared bill of indictments against the prisoner—a provision necessary to legalize the proceedings of every court of justice. The Sanhedrin itself originated the charges against Him. "The Sanhedrin did not and could not originate charges; it only investigated those brought before it," says Edersheim. So this was in direct violation of the Jewish law. The law of witnesses was disregarded (Deut. 17:6 and 19:18, 19). False witnesses were sought to testify against Him, but no true witness was brought in to witness for Him. Jesus was abused, and struck in the mouth during His hearing. The trial was begun and concluded within one day—a flagrant violation of the Jewish law. If a man were convicted on a capital charge, no judgment could be pronounced until the afternoon of the following day. One night must intervene between the verdict and the sentence. In a few short hours our Lord was arrested, twice tried, and executed. Christ was compelled by the high priest to be a witness against Himself, and, upon His own testimony was convicted and condemned, in direct violation of the Jewish law. The members of the Sanhedrin were required, in case of a trial for a capital offense, to vote in turn, beginning with the youngest, but, in direct violation of this law, in the case of Christ, they all cried out their condemnation at once. There was no pretense of a defense.

The Roman trial was as much an outrage as the Jewish one. Jesus was sentenced to death on the charge of blasphemy, but what did Pilate care about blasphemy? There must be a political charge against the prisoner when brought before Pilate, so the cunning priests said, "We found this fellow perverting the nation, and forbidding to give tribute to Caesar, saying that He is Christ, a King" (Luke 23:2). This was a deliberate lie, for Christ had told them to render to Caesar the things that were Caesar's. Jesus stood before Pilate, therefore, charged, not with blasphemy, but with treason against the Roman state. And what was the verdict of the Roman governor? "I find no fault in Him! I will let Him go!" Still the priesthood thirsted for His blood, and brought pressure to bear upon the governor, until finally Pilate, the man of indecision, bluster, subserviency, evasion, protest, compromise, duplicity, and cowardice, against his own knowledge, against his own conscience, to please the people, sent the Man forth to die. In both of these trials, justice was outraged. There was a violation of form in the Jewish trial, and a grosser violation of conscience in the Roman.

Oh, what a trial! Taken before the Sanhedrin unjustly, found guilty of blasphemy, and sentenced to death. Then taken before Pilate, charged with sedition—and acquitted! More than that, taken before Herod, charged with sedition—and acquitted! Brought again before Pilate, charged with sedition—and acquitted! Yet executed!! Executed, not under the charge for which He had been sentenced to death, but under the charge of which He had been three times acquitted!

Our Savior submitted to all this with never a word of protest. When He was buffeted, scourged, spit upon, nailed to the Cross, He showed patience, rather than power. The power would be displayed, and His vindication would come in His resurrection. He could wait. His hour was come, and He yielded Himself to the stroke. From oppression and from judgment He was hurried away.

His Death

This verse goes on with a question: "Who shall declare His generation?" Again translators give a number of meanings, all of which we believe to be true.

One makes this expression to mean, "As to His generation, who shall set it forth?" That is, who can set forth the wickedness, the guilt, of His generation (i. e., His contemporaries), who with "wicked hands" crucified Him?

Another expresses it as "Who shall declare His posterity?" The generations, or descendants of the first Adam are declared to us in Genesis 5; but who shall declare His? Jennings asks, "Where is the progeny that shall carry along His line, and, with it, His claims to the throne of David, His father after the flesh? It expires with Him. That claim is His alone, and it falls to the ground with His death."

Alexander renders these words as follows: "In His generation who will think that He was cut off from the land of the living, for the transgression of my people, as a curse for them?" This means that when the Messiah was cut off for the sins of His people He accomplished a work of which His contemporaries never dreamed.

We may not be dogmatic about any of these translations, but we are sure that none of them contains untruth, and we are positive that these clauses do set forth the fact and the manner of His death. He was "cut off" in the midst of His days, "cut off" with wicked and violent hands. He died on the Cross, but not through the Cross. Humanly speaking, Christ died of a broken heart hours before the crucifixion would have been fatal. Divinely speaking, He died of His own will, when His work was finished, dismissing His own spirit into the hands of His Father.

Underlying all this there was a Divine purpose being worked out. With "wicked hands" men crucified Him, yet He was "delivered by the determinate counsel and foreknowledge of God." Man meant one thing, but God intended another. This purpose of God was unknown to the men of our Lord's generation. The men of His time had no conception of the redemption of the world which was to be effected by His death. The greatest crime that ever stained the annals of our race secured the world's greatest blessing. "For the transgression of my people was He stricken." He was smitten for the sins of the people when they "did esteem Him stricken, smitten of God" (Isaiah 53:4) for His own sins!

The vicarious atoning character of our Lord's sufferings and death is here emphasized. Precisely the same doctrine is here as in II Cor. 5:21: "Him Who knew no sin He made to be sin on our behalf; that we might become the righteousness of God in Him." "Even as the Son of Man came not to be ministered unto, but to minister, and to give His life a ransom for many" (Matt. 20:28). "Christ hath redeemed us from the curse of the law, being made a curse for us" (Gal. 3:13). Our Lord not only suffered from the injustice of man; He suffered also on the Cross from the justice of God —the justice of God manifested in the smiting of our sins, which were laid on Him, for "Jehovah hath laid on Him the iniquity of us all" (Isaiah 53:6). On the Cross, Christ suffered the just penalty of a just God against our sins. God will forgive a sinner, but God can never forgive sins; He is just, and must smite sin. We are saved because Christ was smitten in our stead. As to Israel of old, so with pathos to us today the prophet is saying: "You did esteem Him stricken? Well, He was, but—stricken for you." "Believe on the Lord Jesus Christ and thou shalt be saved" (Acts 16:31).

His Burial

We give a possible translation of the ninth verse: "And they made (or 'appointed') His grave with the wicked, but with a rich man (he was) in His death; although He had done no violence, neither was any deceit in His mouth." They intended Him to be buried with the wicked, but He was interred in the tomb of a rich man, Joseph of Arimathea. Since the

Messiah was to die like a criminal it might be expected that He would be buried with the thieves among whom He was numbered. The denial of an honorable burial was accounted a great ignominy. One writes: "In all countries, I suppose, it has been the rule that persons put to death as criminals have had ignominious sepulchre. Even after death shame has followed them, though after ages have ofttimes reversed the award and built monuments to them." This was especially the case among the Jews. This was the law of the time as stated by Josephus: "He that blasphemeth God, let him be stoned, and let him hang upon a tree all the day, and let him be buried in an ignominious and obscure manner." God gave His Son to a death of shame, but by special intervention saved Him from any further dishonor. Jewish hatred followed Him to the grave, but it did not have the final disposal of that holy Body. The last enemy hand that ever was laid on our Lord—or ever will be—was at the crucifixion. Only hands of affection may touch Him now. Hands of love took Him from the cross and laid Him in a new tomb which had never been defiled with corruptible body. That "Holy Thing" shall not lie in a defiled grave. Some one has said, "He Who came from a virgin womb can be laid only in a virgin tomb." Joseph of Arimathea begged the body of Pilate, and laid it in His own new tomb "wherein was never man yet laid" (John 20:38-42). In His death, as in His life, He was "separate from sinners."

The reason assigned for His honorable burial is this: "He hath done no violence, neither was deceit found in His mouth." This is another guard thrown about His Holy Person. It is another reiteration of His innocence and of His holiness. It is another declaration that His death was for others.

The tomb established the actuality of Christ's death, but more than that, it established the reality of His resurrection. Thank God, the tomb is not the end. His grave never saw corruption. His grave saw the power of death broken. A Man came from that tomb, never to go back again. "I am He that liveth and was dead, and behold, I am alive forevermore" (Rev. 1:18). That tomb saw death, but it saw resurrection life, too! The tomb of Christ brings hope and banishes despair. He Himself said, "Because I live, ye shall live." The grave of Christ makes the grave of our loved one a grave of hope. The tomb of Christ becomes the gate into everlasting life. The death, burial, and resurrection of Christ have to do with our salvation. This is the Gospel by which we are saved (Read I Cor. 15:1-4). Apart from this work of Christ there can be no salvation. Never before His death and resurrection did any man say, "I shall depart to be with the Lord."

We remind you in closing that there is a sense in which our Lord is on trial still. Saint, what is your attitude toward Him? Remember that His disciples, demoralized with fear, had left Him. Two were with Him, but one, the most zealous of them all, denied Him. The other was silent. After His resurrection, however, they were as bold as lions, and willingly laid down their lives for Him. Child of God, what about you? Sinner, what is your attitude? There were witnesses when He was on trial—false witnesses. Enough accusers there, but not one in His defense. Are you still against Him? They cried out, "Away with Him!" Will you receive Him? They cried out, "We have no king but Caesar." Reader, make Him, just now, the King of *your* life.

Chapter VIII

His Mighty Victory

"Yet it pleased the Lord to bruise Him; He hath put Him to grief: when Thou shalt make His soul an offering for sin, He shall see His seed, He shall prolong His days, and the pleasure of the Lord shall prosper in His hands" *(Isaiah 53:10).*

ON THE Cross Jesus Christ was a victim, but in resurrection Jesus Christ was a victor. "The wages of sin is death," and on the Cross He became the substitutionary victim, made sin for us, to suffer the awful death that our sins so justly deserved. But Jesus Christ was not conquered of death, although it seemed that His enemies had triumphed when the grave closed its mouth upon Him. The faith of His disciples collapsed when their Master was laid in the grave. Three days later, however, He came forth in resurrection, triumphant over sin, and death, and the grave, and the Devil.

"Death cannot keep his prey—
    Jesus, my Savior!
He tore the bars away—
    Jesus, my Lord!

"Up from the grave He arose,
With a mighty triumph o'er His foes;
He arose a Victor from the dark domain,
And He lives forever with His saints to reign.
He arose! He arose!
Hallelujah! Christ arose!"

The Victim

The exaltation of the Monarch begins with the tenth verse of Isaiah fifty-three, but the background is black. The somber shadow of the Cross of Calvary falls here. Jesus Christ is "bruised," or "crushed," and put to grief. The bitter experiences of humiliation, rejection, suffering, and death through which our Lord went are set forth in these words. Over and above what wicked men did, when they wrought out the evil in their hearts in nailing Christ to the Cross, we have the fact that "Jehovah was pleased to crush Him." Jesus Christ was sinless and spotless, yet He suffered from Jehovah. "Here is not only the mystery of suffering innocence; but of innocence suffering at the hands of righteousness and perfect love." Why should Jehovah be *pleased* to bruise Him? Why should God, Who has no pleasure in the death of the wicked, be pleased to put the Holy One to grief? Jesus Christ bore this testimony: "I do always those things that please Him" (John 8:29). That this testimony was true was certified by the Father Who spoke from heaven, declaring: "This is My beloved Son, in Whom I am well pleased" (Matt. 3:17; 17:5). "Yet it pleased the Lord to bruise Him!" The "mystery of mysteries" of the agony and death of Christ must remain forever inexplicable were it not for the explanation given by God Himself. Deep in the heart of Jehovah lay this tragedy of a suffering Messiah, hidden for ages. Christ was the Lamb of God, slain even before the foundation of the world. The sufferings of Christ proceeded from the "determinate counsel and foreknowledge of God." Men manifested their enmity toward God by their treatment of His Son, but God "made the sin of men subservient to His pleasure, His will, and predetermined counsel," writes Delitzsch. God not only permitted the Cross; it was His doing, and it "pleased" Him. The prophet did not mean, of course, that Jehovah was pleased with the sufferings of Christ *as such*. That meaning would be an unwarrantable distortion of the prophet's words. The Father did not look with delight upon the death agony of His Son. The pleasure of Jehovah came because of the designed and glorious ends accomplished by the sacrifice of our Savior. It pleased Jehovah to bruise Him in the same sense in which it pleased the Son to do the Father's will. When the shadow of the Cross fell upon our Lord in the garden (a Cross, the meaning of which He so fully knew, and which we so poorly know), He prayed in agony, with sweat like great drops of blood falling down upon the ground, "Father, if Thou be willing, remove this cup from Me; nevertheless, not My will, but Thine, be done" (Luke 22:42-44). Even so, the Father shrank with anguish from bruising the Son, and putting His Son to grief. Yet, in spite of the agony, the Son delighted to do the will of the Father, and, in spite of the anguish, the Father was pleased to bruise the Son. Why? In both cases, because the cross-bearing work of Christ was the only way to achieve the joy, the blessing, the perpetuity of man's redemption. God has revealed Himself as a God of justice and righteousness, as well as a God of love. Sin must be punished under God's justice, if salvation is to be attained under God's love. Kuldell says: "God can as little divest Himself of His punitive justice as He can of His saving love. Justice and mercy are two arms of the same heart, willing and planning the salvation of the race. And since transgression has entered into our life as a disturbing element, punishment and suffering had to be introduced both for atonement and for discipline." The very fact that Jehovah was pleased to smite Him is proof that He is pleased to save us. He was bruised in our stead. The justice of God was satisfied by sending His only Son to Calvary, that the love of God might triumph in bringing many sons unto glory. When Isaac lay bound upon the altar, ready to be slain, it was Abraham's will to see Isaac die, not because there was any wrath in the father, but because there was a submissive desire to see God's will accomplished. As Abraham surrendered his only son to death out of love to God, so the Father in heaven yielded His Only Begotten to the death of the Cross out of love to man. Paul Gerhardt, in his beautiful Passion Hymn, "Lamb Bears All the Guilt Away," sings of Jehovah saying to the Messiah:

> "Go forth, My Son, redeem to Thee
> The children who're exposed by Me
> To punishment and anger.
> The punishment is great, and dread
> The wrath, but Thou Thy Blood shall shed
> And free them from this danger."

"When Thou (God) shalt make His soul an offering for sin" has been variously translated as, "When Thou shalt make His soul a guilt-offering;" "When His soul shall make an offering;" "When His soul has been made an offering; "When He presents His soul a trespass offering." Probably the translation to be preferred is the one that makes the Servant offer His own life, since, as David Baron says, Jehovah is nowhere else addressed in this chapter. This does not preclude the fact that the Father offered the Son, for we must predicate to the Father the actions that are predicated to the Son, since "I and My Father are One." "All was settled in the Divine counsel from all eternity, and when the ideal became the actual, God the Father wrought with God the Son to effectuate it." The Messiah's dying work was a glorious act of self-surrender. He gave His life as an offering for the sin of others and took upon Himself the penalty which their guilt had incurred. It was by the Father's appointment, yet it was none the less the Son's own act. "God so loved the world that He *gave* His Son" (John 3:16). "The Son of God Who loved me and *gave* Himself for me" (Galatians 2:20).

72

Jesus Christ offered His soul a *trespass offering*, as "offering for sin" should be rendered. This term comes to us from the Mosaic economy, with its ceremonial institutions, and is included in the five offerings which cover practically every offering that Israel ever brought to God—the burnt, the meal, the peace, the sin, and the trespass offerings (Leviticus chapters 1-7). The trespass offering was very closely related to the sin offering, with much in common between the two. The sinful nature of man was cared for by the sin offering; the sinful acts of man by the trespass offering. Both root and fruit of sin were looked to in these offerings. The sin offering conveyed the idea of propitiation; the trespass offering that of satisfaction. The sin offering had its aspect God-ward; the trespass offering rather looked man-ward. In the sin offering the offerer recognized his sacrifice as a substitute God-ward, while in the trespass offering there was the added thought of compensation man-ward, "to make amends for the harm that he hath done." The ritual of the sin offering symbolized the "bearing away" of sin; that of the trespass offering symbolized purification, or cleansing from sin. Every offering, no matter which we consider, finds its glorious fullness in Jesus Christ. It was the one supreme sacrifice, the Lamb of God, that God was setting forth in the various sin offerings of the Old Testament; and since they were all fulfilled in Him, they have ceased forever. Now we say, "Behold the Lamb of God that taketh away the sin of the world!" It is the blood of Jesus Christ which "cleanseth us from all sin." "There is therefore now no condemnation to them which are in Christ Jesus." Thus all the ground is covered by the one great sacrifice, and nothing is left undone.

The offering which Jesus Christ made was His soul, His life, His all—*Himself*. "I gave, I gave Myself for thee." In the old covenant sacrifices, life was *taken*; here, the life was *given*. He could give no more. He brought His soul, His whole self, a sacrifice for our sin; the Father is satisfied, and we are saved. This is the New Covenant. We are accepted in the Beloved. The offering of His soul was appropriate towards God, and efficient for man.

We quote this truth from Clemance: "We may well look on with profound reverence as the Most High brings out, in ritual, prophecy, and gospel, that truth which men are most ready to let slip; viz., *the exceeding sinfulness of sin*! In gospel, prophecy, and ritual, there is, in order to meet the world's need, not only a central figure, but a central fact. In the ritual—the priest and the offering. In the prophecy —the Messiah and His offering. In the Gospel—the Christ and His offering. Here is a three-fold cord, 'not easily broken.' Never let us forget the double aspect of the work of Christ—large enough to cover all the ground; minute enough to point out me and to save me!"

The Victor

"He shall see His seed." Now we pass from the gloom to the glory. We look now at the mighty victory of our Lord over sin and death. The closing words of this verse give us the resurrection of Christ, and the blessed results that follow. *"He shall see His seed,"* or, more literally, "a seed," or "posterity." The grain of wheat fell into the ground to die, but now it bringeth forth much fruit. Here is the answer to the question, "Who shall declare His generation?" or "Who shall tell His posterity?" His pains on the Cross were birth pangs, "the travail of His soul," out of which was begotten a numerous spiritual offspring. His seed is the company of the redeemed gathering round Him, owing their life to His death. He is the Head of a new creation, a new spiritual race. Adam is the head of the human family, Christ is the Head of spiritual seed. That spiritual progeny is in existence today, part on earth, part in heaven. It is the company redeemed, not with silver and gold, but with the precious blood

of our Lord. It is the company that believes on the Lord Jesus Christ. No boundaries of man's devising can enclose it. Who can number it? It is a mighty host moving on to certain victory. Yet the meaning of this prophecy, "He shall see His seed," we so dimly discern! We just glimpse the glory now, but in that day when God shall wipe away all tears from our eyes; when there shall be no more death, neither sorrow nor crying; when God shall have hushed all the jarring conflicts which distress us now; when we shall be caught up yonder to see our Lord, and to be with Him, and to be like Him; when we shall hear Him say, "This is what I intended when I died for thee"; when we shall stand among the unnumbered company of the redeemed—then we shall see the joy of our Savior fulfilled in the "bringing of many sons unto glory," and we shall know by actual experience the fullness of the bliss and beauty of this prophecy: "He shall see His seed." "But thanks be to God, which giveth us the victory through our Lord Jesus Christ" (I Cor. 15:57).

> "His be the Victor's name
> Who fought the fight alone;
> Triumphant saints no honor claim,
> His conquest was their own."

"He shall prolong His days." This is in seeming contradiction to the statement made in this same chapter, verse 8, that He should be "cut off" out of the land of the living, and more surprising, as the Pulpit Commentary notes, because His death is made the condition of this long life: "When His soul has been made an offering for sin," then "He shall prolong His days." He was to die, and to be buried, yet He is to "prolong His days." This apparent discrepancy is reconciled by the facts of His resurrection after His death on the Cross and His burial in the rich man's tomb. He was not only "delivered for our offenses; He was raised again for our justification" (Rom. 4:25). Christ died, but He rose. He

lives, never again to die. "I am He that liveth, and was dead; and, behold, I am alive forevermore." This is in accord with the prophecy of the Messiah in Psalm 16: "Thou wilt not leave My soul in hell (Sheol); neither wilt Thou suffer Thine Holy One to see corruption. Thou wilt shew Me the path of life: in Thy presence is fulness of joy."

Christ is not here. He entered within the veil. He appears now in the presence of God for us. The case of "His seed" is in His hands. "Wherefore He is able also to save them to the uttermost that come unto God by Him, seeing He ever liveth to make intercession for them" (Heb. 7:26). "And if any man sin we have an Advocate with the Father, Jesus Christ the Righteous" (I John 2:1). His work on Calvary's Cross is to be brought to a consummation by His glorious after-life. In His hands is lodged the whole of redemption's work, down to the end of time. He is our great High Priest. He is not a priest after the order of the Aaronic priesthood. Under the Mosaic dispensation a man might be unfit for the office, or unequal to it, yet he was in that office for life, not because he was fitted for it, but because he was appointed to it. On the other hand, he might be well fitted for the office, administering the affairs of the people of God with the utmost skill, and care and devotion, yet the hand of death would end his priesthood. These defects do not mar the priesthood of our Lord. He is "without sin"; He is "perfect"; He "liveth forever." The effect of His unchanging and unending priesthood is a redemption that is unvarying and unending. Such a redemption we have. Thank God, our Savior has "length of days forever and ever."

The tenth verse begins: "It pleased the Lord to bruise Him," and ends: *"The pleasure of the Lord shall prosper in His hand."* This means that Jehovah had a purpose in bruising Him, and that that purpose shall have a triumphant accomplishment. The "pleasure of the Lord" is the salvation of the lost.

(Read of His good pleasure in Col. 1:19-22.) "Shall prosper" means that it shall be carried out to the end. "In His hand" means "by His instrumentality." Our Lord has the fulfillment of Jehovah's designs entrusted entirely to Him, and He will not pause until He has completely accomplished them.

> "And Jehovah's good pleasure
> In His hand shall go forward,
> In triumph increasing."—Jennings.

"Christ crucified" is the preaching that God is pleased to use to save them that believe (I Cor. 1:21-25). The saving of men by His grace has been going on through the centuries. From east and from west, from north and from south, men are coming to fall at the foot of Christ's Cross, to receive there a welcome into the household of God, and so "the pleasure of the Lord" prospers.

Have you, reader, ever taken a stand at the foot of the Cross, to contemplate Christ pouring out His soul unto death, to provide a ransom for you? "Greater love hath no man than this, that a man lay down His life for His friend." But you were not His friend. "The mind of the flesh is enmity against God." No sacrifice can match Christ's for He died for His enemies, for the weak, for the ungodly. The sinless Son of God took the place of sinners, who hated Him, and suffered their merited stroke, that the penalty of sin might not be theirs. Have you contemplated the Cross? Study it again, for you will never find its match in the history of the universe of God.

A young lady, a novice in art, said to her father, who was an accomplished man of taste, "Father, I cannot enjoy the works of the old masters."

"Then," said he, "look at them till you can."

Do you appreciate the Cross? It stands peerless and alone. This is the place where Christ endured the separation from God which we deserved, that we might enjoy the nearness to God which He deserved.

Study it until your soul is overwhelmed with the mystery, the majesty, the marvel, the measure, the might of it. There is not in heaven or earth such an amazing wonder as this! All the promises of God are centered in that Cross. All the happiness and good of man are centered in that Cross. Here the vilest sinner, the moment he receives Christ by faith, is accepted of God. Come to the Cross with your poverty, and get His prosperity. "If He is your physician, you shall have health. If He is your bread, you shall never hunger. If He is your fountain of life, you shall never thirst. If He is your light, you shall never abide in darkness. If He is your joy, you shall not remain in sorrow. If He is your truth, you shall not be led astray. If He is your righteousness, who shall condemn you? If He is your sanctification, who shall reject you? If He is your acquittal, who shall sentence you? If He is for you, who shall be against you?" Come to the Cross with your death, and get His life. Come to the Cross with your ruin, and get His perfection. Come to the Cross with your sin, and get His righteousness. Come to the Cross with your darkness, and get His light. Come to the Cross with your sorrow and get His joy.

Then shall man be happy, and "the pleasure of the Lord shall prosper in His hand."

"Lamb of God, Thou now art seated
    High upon Thy Father's throne,
All Thy gracious work completed,
    All Thy mighty vict'ry won."

Chapter 9

His Merited Satisfaction

*"He shall see of the travail of His Soul, and
shall be satisfied: by His knowledge shall My
Righteous Servant justify many; for He shall
bear their iniquities" (Isaiah 53:11).*

ATISFIED! Our Savior shall be satisfied!
This truth ought to fill the heart of the child
of God with joy. Our joy over the victory of
the Lord ought to be greater than over our
inheritance in the Lord. Isaiah fifty-three pictures the
sufferings of the Savior for sinners; but in the end it
shows multitudes born to Him through those sufferings—multitudes who share His life, who show forth
His death, who proclaim His praises, who are arrayed
in His righteousness, who are His delight.

The Satisfaction of the Savior

"He shall see of the travail of His soul, and shall
be satisfied." The Hebrew word which is here translated "travail" is used about sixty times in the Old
Testament, and means trouble of any kind, or trouble
of many kinds. It is also translated "toil," "labour,"
"sorrow," "grievance," all of which indicate that it
means strong effort, attended by pain and grief.

It is the "travail of His soul." His sufferings were
more than physical. Had His sufferings been physical
only, He would have died as many a martyr has, with
a shout of triumph, with the face of an angel, even
as Stephen. Martyrs do not die bewildered, dazed, undone, crying: "My God, my God, why hast Thou
forsaken me?" Our Lord's suffering was an intense

suffering of the soul. Culross observes that this travail of His soul includes "all the toil, suffering, and sorrow through which He came, and has been outlined, if not unfolded, in the previous part of the prophecy. It culminates when He was cut off out of the land of the living, and His soul was made an offering for sin, accomplishing what the Levitical sacrifices only symbolized. No accumulation of mere bodily sufferings could satisfy these expressions. The 'travail' is that of the soul; it has its seat within, and is such as might find voice in those words reported from Gethsemane, 'My soul is exceeding sorrowful, even unto death,' or in those words reported from the Cross, 'My God, My God, why hast Thou forsaken Me?' It is what the Greek litany calls 'unknown agonies'." Jesus Christ came from the bosom of the Father, the purest thing in the whole universe of God, and we cannot understand His "travail" when the overwhelming wickedness of the world pierced His pure soul.

A number of Christian commentators paraphrase these words as follows, using the thought expressed in the preceding verse (10): "He shall see His seed; He shall be satisfied with length of days." This is true, of course, but without doubt the meaning goes far beyond this. Alexander's translation reads: "From the labour of His soul He shall see, He shall be satisfied"; and another makes it, "He shall look out from the travail of His soul." That is, He shall be satisfied, not only with the results of His sufferings, but with the reason for the sufferings. He shall be satisfied, not *after* His sufferings only, but *in* them. He shall be satisfied, not only when the outcome of His work is complete, but satisfied with His mission on earth, even when in the very depths of His sufferings.

Jesus Christ was satisfied in His suffering, knowing that it was for the salvation of sinners. "What a Friend we have in Jesus!" He stepped into the place of the sinner—our place—to take the burden of our sin upon Himself, that it might be flung away forever. He bowed His soul to death that we might be raised to life. He was numbered among the sinners, that we might be numbered among the saints. Sufferings should have been meted out to us because of our sins, but salvation is meted out to us because of His sacrifice. Salvation is not of our merit; salvation is of His mercy. We as sinners should have suffered; He as Savior suffered for us. He knew the satisfaction that comes from suffering to shield another. There is no satisfaction for those who are self-centered. He never would have been satisfied had not His Cross provided a highway to life, a gateway to glory.

In one of the battles of the Civil War, a Union officer lay wounded before the wall of a southern city. The firing was so fierce that his comrades could not remove him, and there he lay between two contending armies. The poison of his wounds and the scorching rays of the southern sun caused his blood to boil with consuming fever. "Water, water!" he cried, "for God's sake, water!" A lieutenant of the Confederate army said to his comrades: "Boys, I have a mind to go down and take that fellow some water." "Don't you do that," they begged, "you would not live a moment, if you put your head above the wall."

"No, I suppose it is not best," he replied, and so the firing went on. Then came another heart-rending cry from the wounded man:

"Water, for God's sake, won't somebody bring me some water?"

The lieutenant's eyes filled with tears and he said:

"Boys, I can't stand that. I'm going to take that fellow some water if I die in the attempt." Filling his canteen, he strapped it to his side. Tying a handkerchief to his bayonet, he raised it above the wall, hoping that the Union soldiers would regard it as a flag of truce and stop firing for a moment, but they paid no attention to it. Climbing over the wall where the bullets were flying as thick as hail, he went down to the wounded man, and holding the canteen to his mouth, gave him all the cool water he could drink. Then bracing him with a knapsack under his shoulders, he put the canteen against his breast so that he could help himself as often as he wished—and clambered up the fortification amid the shouts of both armies.

Man in his sin is like the wounded officer on the battlefield. The fever in his soul is burning, and there is no one to help. Christ never would have been satisfied had He not come down from the battlements of heaven to save us. "The Son of Man came not to be ministered unto but to minister, and to give His life a ransom for many" (Mark 10:45).

Suppose that wounded man had refused the water that the soldier had brought at the risk of life? Had he not deserved to perish? The answer is plain. Do not refuse the refreshing draught of the Lord's salvation. Drink at His hand. The Savior's suffering is the only source of the sinner's satisfaction.

Jesus Christ was satisfied in His suffering, knowing that it was for the vindication of God's righteousness. When sin entered the world, it called for the manifestation of God's righteousness. A "just God" must punish sin. Yet for 4,000 years God "covered" sin, "passed over" sin, "winked at" sin. Surely the sacrifice of bulls and goats could never glorify the righteousness of God. There must be such an adequate vindication of the righteousness of God that forgiveness of sin could never be confounded with connivance at it. There must be a public condemnation of sin. In a voluntary act, to meet the need of guilty man, and to display the justice of God, Christ offered Himself, without spot or blemish, as sacrifice for sin. He stood before the universe, charged with the sins of the human race, and their consequence. He was identified with sin, to the end that He was bruised between the millstones of God's justice. His holy soul was pierced with human guilt. He tasted death for every man. Christ died for our sins. This is the only way in which God might "declare His righteousness," and still be the "Justifier of him who believeth in Jesus" (Rom. 3:25, 26). So Christ saw of the "travail of His soul," and was satisfied.

Jesus Christ was satisfied in His suffering, knowing that it was for the manifestation of God's love. There cannot be love for sinning souls without travail. The wounds of Christ cry out His love for us—God's love for us. God's interest in humanity is summed up in the great statement, "God is love." God's relation to the Divine Son is expressed in forms of infinite tenderness: "The Only Begotten Son, which is in the bosom of the Father"; "The Father loveth the Son." The mystery and power of the love of God for the sinner are set forth in "God so loved the world that He gave His only Begotten Son, that whosoever believeth on Him should not perish, but have everlasting life;" "He Who spared not His own Son, but freely delivered Him up for us all." The Cross of Calvary is the perfect expression of the love of God. When we say that God is love, we can prove it by the Cross. When we look at nature we see, not love, but a groaning and travailing in pain, and in the human race we see the same sorrow and pain, but when we turn to Calvary we see in the travailing soul of the Son of God the very weft of love. At the Cross the heart of God is made bare to us. At Calvary God is not robed with clouds and darkness, but with the vesture of sacrificial love. If you never before believed that God loves you, you must believe when you take your stand at the foot of the Cross, to see the Savior suffering for your sins. Fall at the foot of that Cross and confess Him, "My Lord and my God."

Jesus Christ was satisfied in His suffering, knowing that it was for the destruction of the Devil's works. "For this purpose the Son of God was manifested, that He might destroy the works of the Devil" (I John 3:8). Just what is involved in this we do not fully know, but we shall, in that day when the mists have rolled away. The curse of sin will be gone; grace will abound where sin and death reigned, and man will be lifted up to a position and perfection that Adam never knew. Even now Satan is a defeated enemy.

Jesus Christ was satisfied in His suffering, knowing that it was for his own perfection as Savior. "For it became Him, for Whom are all things, and by Whom are all things, in bringing many sons unto glory, to make the Captain of their salvation perfect through sufferings" (Heb. 2:10). Some one asks, "But was Jesus Christ not perfect before He went to the Cross?" Yes, perfect morally, for from the moment of His conception He was "that Holy Thing," but He could not be a perfect Savior apart from sufferings, since the government of God necessitated the punishment of sin. Jesus Christ by His sufferings laid a righteous foundation for the salvation of sinners. Only by His sufferings could He lead "many sons to glory."

So Christ was satisfied when in His sufferings, because He knew the results secured by His sufferings. His satisfaction was justified by the efficiency of His sacrifice.

If our Lord found satisfaction in the hour of His sufferings, think how much greater must be the satisfaction when the sufferings have passed, and the glory has been secured. "He shall look out from the travail of His soul, and shall be satisfied." "Look out" as from a watch tower; "look out" to the far issues of His sufferings; "look out" to the glory that should follow, and so He would be satisfied to bear His sufferings.

Jesus Christ is the prophet like unto Moses, and when Moses was about to die, he "went up from the plains of Moab unto the mountain of Nebo, to the top of Pisgah, that is over against Jericho. And the Lord showed him all the land of Gilead, unto Dan, and all Naphtali, and the land of Ephraim, and Manasseh, and all the land of Judah unto the utmost sea, and the south, and the plain of the valley of Jericho, the city of palm trees, unto Zoar" (Deut. 34:1-3). Moses endured the wilderness wanderings, with suffering, weariness and pain, to bring this people out of the slavery of Egypt and into the land of Canaan. Now, as "his eye swept over the matchless panorama of verdure and fruitfulness, the blue of distant mountains, whose clefts in the afternoon sun seemed inlaid with sapphire and emerald; as he saw the flashing of distant waters and the waving of tall, eastern trees aslant in the glow," we believe that he was satisfied, and that the glories of the land he saw were compensation for all the sufferings he had endured. Our Savior looked out from the travail of His soul to see the new heavens and the new earth, wherein dwelleth righteousness. Moses must have had a fulness of joy in that day when he stood in Canaan with his Lord. Surely our Lord will have a fulness of joy in that day when He is in the midst of the host of the redeemed, in that sinless, new creation.

Hebrews speaks of the same satisfaction of our Lord in these words: "Who for the joy that was set before Him, endured the Cross, despising the shame, and is set down at the right hand of the throne of God" (Heb. 12:2). Clemance, in speaking of this satisfaction and joy of our Savior, says: "It will be the joy of the *Sufferer* Whose agony is forgotten in the abundance of bliss—the joy of the *Sower* in reaping the abundance of the harvest—the joy of the *Shepherd* in seeing all the sheep as one flock, safe forever in the heavenly fold—the joy of the *Friend* in seeing all His friends by His side in a union with Him and with each other that no misapprehension shall ever mar, and no sin shall ever stain—it will be the joy of the *Leader* Who has brought all His host into the promised land—it will be the joy of the *Mediator,* Who has discharged His trust and surrendered it to the Father, saying, "Of those whom Thou gavest Me

I have lost none"—it will be the joy of the *King* Who is to reign forever over a kingdom in which revolt has been made impossible through the achievements of almighty grace—it will be the joy of the *Redeemer* when the redemption is complete, fulfilling His longings and His prayers—it will be the joy of the *Firstborn Son* at seeing every member of the new-born family safe in a happy home, which no sin can disturb, and no death invade—it will be the joy of the *Son of Man* in witnessing the ideal of human perfection—it will be the joy of the *Son of God,* as to principalities and powers in heavenly places He reveals through a glorified church the manifold wisdom of God, showing to worlds on worlds what Infinite Love devised and Infinite Power achieved! Then, then, will be the consummation of the joy, when Christ shall look back on the travail of His soul, and HIS REST SHALL BE GLORIOUS!"

> "Waiting till His royal banner
> Floateth far and wide.
> Till He see of His travail—
> Satisfied."

The Justification of the Sinner

"By His knowledge shall my Righteous Servant justify many," is given as a literal translation by David Baron as, "By His knowledge shall make righteous (bring righteousness) the Righteous One (My Servant) many." This prophetic teaching blends with the apostolic teaching as set forth in Rom. 5:19: "By the obedience of One shall many be made righteous."

We have here the "One" set over against the "many." The "One" is the "Righteous One," while the "many" are unrighteous. The "One" is the "Righteous One" while the "many" need to be made righteous.

There is no question as to Who the "One" is. Benjamin Wills Newton states that this "One" stands in a sphere of His own; that He held in earth a position of righteousness that was singular and isolated, and that there was none other like Him; Newton declares that the very formation of the Hebrew passage emphasizes this. Baron also states that the "construction of the phrase is unusual, and is intended to emphasize the unique character of the Servant of Jehovah." "There has been but One in all history to Whom this expression could completely and unreservedly apply." Jesus Christ was inherently righteous. Jesus Christ was not tempted in all points like as we are—He was "in all points tempted like as we are, APART FROM SIN." Jesus Christ was not two persons, but one Person with two natures. Jesus Christ was "God manifest in the flesh." God cannot sin. To add to Jesus Christ a personality capable of sinning is to add another person to the Godhead, thereby changing the Trinity to a quartette. Or else it means the subtraction of a person from the Trinity, for if Christ could sin, He is not the second Person of the Trinity. In either case, this amounts to an annihilation of the Trinity. To annihilate the Trinity is to annihilate Deity. We need to remember again that when we speak of the Virgin Birth we are not speaking about the birth of a mere babe, but about the INCARNATION. Thank God, "in Him is no sin."

On the other hand we have "the many," the great mass of mankind. This Scripture indicates their great need—the need of justification. *We* are included in "the many." We are conscious of sin. The last part of this verse, "He shall bear their iniquities" indicates our condition—we are laden with iniquities. Surely we need no proof of this, except our own hearts. If so, put yourself over against the Son of God, the "Righteous One," and you will see how short of the glory of God you have come. Or put yourself over against the Law of God. "The Law of the Lord is perfect," and if you would know how unperfect (more than imperfect!) you are, examine yourself honestly in the light of its perfections, and you will find that "by the law is the knowledge of sin." Sin is always disobedience to the Divine law, rebellion against the Divine will. We have lost our true relation to God through sin. If we need to be set right, it is because we are not right. If we need justification, it is because there is a charge hanging over us. If the law is the highest expression of the *will* of God, its violation must call forth the highest expression of the *wrath* of God. So we read of the sinner that "the wrath of God abideth upon him."

We shall look for a moment at the word "justify." In our text justification means to treat, to account, to regard, to declare, or to pronounce righteous in the eyes of the law. Justification is not concerned with our spiritual condition, but with our legal position. Justification is more than forgiveness of sins. A *criminal* may be pardoned, but he cannot be declared righteous; a *Christian* is not only pardoned, but also declared righteous. Man can forgive his fellowman, but he cannot justify him. God can do both. Forgiveness is only negative, the removal of condemnation; justification is also positive, the bestowal of righteousness. Forgiveness is being stripped; justification is being clothed. Justification means that, in the sight of God, the *sinful* man is regarded as a *sinless* man. Sin brings separation from God; justification results in reinstatement before God. The Savior came to accept the sinner's standing, that the sinner might receive the Savior's standing. "How great is the privilege, how transcendent the honor, when through the One standing in the room of the many, the many can stand in the place of the One!"

But the ordinary sense of the word "justify" is not sufficient here, for it bears the ethical sense of "making righteous." I think that we are safe in saying that in the New Testament we will always find associated with justification a positive moral work within the life of the believer. The justified man is not only acquitted from condemnation of sin and declared righteous; he is also actually "made righteous." Jesus Christ by His death sets believers before the throne of God in the righteousness of God, but He also by the gift of the indwelling Spirit causes them to lead righteous lives. As saved people, we are called upon to yield the members of our bodies unto God as "instruments of righteousness."

The ground of our justification is indicated by the title of our Lord Jesus Christ used here by Jehovah—"My Servant." It is the result of His "service." Our justification is brought about through the finished work of our Lord. He was in the "form of God," but took upon Him the "form of a Servant," that He might become "obedient unto death, yea, the death of the Cross." This is what the Spirit had in mind when the prophet wrote, "He shall bear their iniquities." He wrote it before, in verse 6, "Jehovah hath laid on Him the iniquity of us all." There is no excuse to mistake or doubt the basis of our justification, for the truth is set forth very clearly. *"He* shall bear *their* iniquities" makes a virtual antithesis, suggesting the idea of exchange or mutual substitution. They shall receive His righteousness; He shall bear their iniquities. Even so it is written, "He Who knew no sin was made sin for us, that we might become the righteousness of God in Him" (II Cor. 5:21). Dr. W. H. Griffith-Thomas writes: "This doctrine of justification because of the work of Christ is seen all through the New Testament. Our Lord's perfect obedience, even unto death, His payment of the penalty due to to our transgressions, His spotless righteousness, the entire merit of His Divine Person and work, form the ground or basis of our justification. This merit is reckoned to us, put to our account; God looks at us in Him, not only as pardoned, but as righteous...It is sometimes stated that this theory is not found in Scripture, because of its association with what is sometimes called 'legal fiction,' but in the light of the teaching of the New Testament on our Lord's atoning death, by which we are accounted righteous before God, the doctrine of imputation is quite clear, and is taught plainly in Scripture, and therefore in the truest theology."

Sins are not justified, but the sinner is. Sins are condemned, not condoned. In order that the sinner may be delivered *from* his sins, the Savior was delivered *for* his sins (Rom. 4:25). When Christ hung on the Cross our sins were in the Divine contemplation laid on Him, that we might be free from all condemnation. "There is therefore now no condemnation to them which are in Christ Jesus." Only the sinner is under condemnation—"He that believeth not is condemned." The sinner is not under condemnation because he is a great sinner, for Christ is a great Savior Who died for great sinners. The sinner is under the condemnation of God because of his rejection of the Son of God.

The method of justification is also set forth in this phrase: "By His knowledge shall My righteous Servant justify many." "By His knowledge" means either (1) the knowledge which He possesses, as in John 17:25, Matt. 11:27; or (2) the knowledge of Him, as in John 17:3. Although both are true, nearly all authorities give preference to the latter meaning—the knowledge of Him on the part of others. Alexander says that this is the only satisfactory meaning in the light of the construction of the phrase, and that it means a "practical experimental knowledge, involving faith and a self-appropriation of the Messiah's righteousness." The merit of the Lord becomes ours by faith. "Faith cometh by hearing," always. Trust answers to truth. It is by knowledge of "Him." As Hooker once said, "God doth justify the believing man, yet not for the worthiness of his belief, but for His worthiness Who is believed." Thomas says, "We are not justified by belief in Christ, but by Christ in Whom we believe." He is the object of our faith. Our hearts say, "Amen!" when we hear

> "My hope is built on nothing less
> Then Jesus' blood and righteousness."

We have again tried to present the Gospel. We have again declared Christ. Now let your faith lay hold on Him Who is the Son of God, the Savior of men. The moment you do that you are saved. The moment you do that you are justified. The moment you do that you are "made righteous." And the moment you realize that your relations as to sinful man are righteously restored to God through the work of the Righteous One, you will have the ground for assurance, and you will become the possessor of the peace that passeth all understanding.

> "I have no refuge of my own,
> But fly to what the Lord hath done,
>   And suffered once for me.
>
> "Slain in the guilty sinner's stead,
> His spotless righteousness I plead,
>   And His availing blood.
>
> "That righteousness my robe shall be,
> That merit shall atone for me,
>   And bring me near to God."

Chapter X

His Matchless Ministry

*"Therefore will I divide Him a portion with
the great, and He shall divide the spoil with
the strong; because He hath poured out His
soul unto death: and He was numbered with
the transgressors; and He bare the sin of
many, and made intercession for the transgressors" (Isaiah 53:12).*

THE SON of Man came not to be ministered
unto, but to minister, and to give His life a
ransom for many," our Lord declared concerning Himself. He is the Monarch with
the matchless ministry. And what a ministry! It has
caused millions of earth to rejoice, and the corridors
of heaven will eternally ring with the praise of it.
He was despised and rejected of men; He was smitten and afflicted of God; He was a Man of sorrows
and acquainted with grief; He was numbered with
the transgressors and cut off out of the land of the
living—all this and much more is included in His
ministry for us. His humiliation and death were His
glory, for they were vicarious throughout—they were
for you and for me. He went through shame to victory; He went through death to life. His life was
cut off, but His work was completed. Surely we
must bow before Him, lips dumb with amazement,
hearts filled with adoration, and confess that

> "Love so amazing, so Divine,
> Demands my life, my soul, my all."

Compensation for the Ministry

The twelfth verse of Isaiah 53 is one from which

we may draw a number of truths, some of which follow:

We see in it the truth of Christ's glorious award. The word "because" in this text has been translated by some "instead of," "inasmuch," "since," "in return for that," expressing the idea of compensation or reward. A glorious reward is bestowed upon Him because of the great redemption accomplished by Him. This reward is given to the Servant by Jehovah—"I will divide Him a portion with the great, and He shall divide the spoil with the strong." Hengstenberg translates this: "I will give Him the mighty for a portion." The Septuagint Version reads: "He shall inherit many." Luther makes it: "I will give Him a great multitude for booty." Jennings renders it: "I will give Him a portion in many," and explains, "The many are not those who share with this unrivaled Servant, but are themselves the objects apportioned to Him." David Baron states that "the *many* who form His portion include not only His own nation, whom He saves and blesses, and who shall yet render Him such loyal devotion and service as the world has not known, but extends beyond the bounds of Israel to the Gentile nations." Many whose guilt He bore shall be His possession. His reward shall be not merely among the few and the feeble, but among the many and the mighty. He shall see His seed. He shall be satisfied.

We see in it the truth of Christ's spiritual triumph. Alexander and others believe that "spiritual triumphs must be here intended, because no other could be represented as the fruit of voluntary humiliation and vicarious suffering." One, in comment, says that this "is figurative language expressive of full victory, and it here means that Christ, by His death, delivers from Satan, the Strong One, mankind that was his spoil." Our Lord spoke of Satan as "a strong man" in the parable He used when accused of casting out demons through the power of Beelzebub. He ridiculed the idea of Satan opposing himself. How can Satan cast out Satan? "How can one enter into a strong man's house, and spoil his goods, except he first bind the strong man? and then he will spoil his house" (Matt. 12:24-30). The strong one in this parable is Satan. The Stronger One Who overcomes him is Christ.

Sinners are slaves of Satan even as the Israelites were slaves of Pharaoh. The sinner is led captive of the Devil. Satan is the "prince of the power of the air, the spirit that now worketh in the children of disobedience." His subjects are bound with the chains of sin. He deceiveth the whole world, and exerts over men a usurped sway. But Christ is the Stronger One. He is the Deliverer from the power of the Devil. Satan has been defeated by our Savior.

(1) We have deliverance from Satan through what Christ *has done* for us. Christ was in the "form of God," but He became Incarnate as the second Man, the last Adam, to overthrow the enemy and deliver the captives. Jesus Christ met Satan in the wilderness and worsted him there, but His great triumph came through His death and resurrection. On the Cross our sins were laid upon Him, and He suffered the judgment that was their due, completing the work of redemption with the cry, "It is finished!" The "Amen!" of the Father to that cry was the resurrection of Christ from the dead. The death and resurrection of Christ constitute the Gospel by which we are saved (I Cor. 15:1-4). He loved us and "loosed us from our sins by His blood." The captives of Satan have been freed from the chains of sin through the "cross-work" of the Savior.

(2) We have deliverance from Satan through what Christ *is doing* for us. After Christ had borne the sins of the world He went on high to begin a priestly ministry for His own. He ever liveth to make intercession for them. If we sin, we have an Advocate with the Father, Jesus Christ the Righteous. He keeps the feet of His saints. But Christ is not only

our Intercessor, He is also our Indweller, for it is "Christ in you, the hope of glory." Through Christ, men come to God, and through him, God comes to men. Human redemption has been accomplished by the triune God through the Son, and when the Son enters into the life of a redeemed man, all the power of God—Father, Son, and Spirit—is manifested in the operation of the spiritual life of that redeemed one. If we are in harmony with indwelling Deity, and He is for us, who can be against us? Satan's Victor is our victory.

(3) We have deliverance from Satan through what Christ *shall do* for us. He shall some day receive us unto Himself. He shall make us like unto Himself (Phil. 3:20, 21). He shall take Satan in hand in that coming day. Satan shall be bound in the bottomless pit, and still later shall be cast into the lake of fire. This shall mark his end. Thank God, we have a present victory over Satan, but we shall have a further complete and eternal deliverance from him.

In this sense, too—the sense of our salvation—we may be said to participate with Him when He divides "the spoil."

We see in it the truth of Christ's political greatness.

One explains this verse as follows: "Jehovah gives Him victory as a great ruler of mankind because of His willing sacrifice." The Cambridge Bible thinks that future political greatness "is certainly suggested." One day heaven shall cry, "The Lord God Omnipotent reigneth!" and He shall come to take His place on earth as King of kings and Lord of lords. He Himself will rule. He will rule in righteousness. He will rule with a rod of iron. He will dash in pieces and break all opposition as a potter's vessel. He will put down all rule and all authority. He alone shall be exalted in that day. His reign will be one of righteousness and law. He is King of the Jews. He is King of the nations.

Again we see our participation with Him, for He

shall divide "the spoil." We shall be partners with Him in His kingdom and glory.

"And with Him all the ransomed seed
Shall reign in that glad day."

We see in it the truth of Christ's universal acknowledgment. Some believe that this verse takes us beyond the mere reign of Christ on earth to a time when He shall be universally confessed and worshipped. The "therefore" of the prophet is made to correspond with the "wherefore" of the apostle. "Wherefore God also hath highly exalted Him, and given Him a name which is above every name: that at the name of Jesus every knee should bow, of beings in heaven, and beings in earth, and beings under the earth; and that every tongue should confess that Jesus Christ is Lord, to the glory of God the Father" (Phil. 2:9-11). He has a name above every name. No other being in the universe bears a name approximating it in glory. One day the beings of the whole universe will bow before Him, and every tongue shall confess that the Man Christ Jesus is Jehovah. Clemance writes: "There are three classes of beings here named: beings in heaven—even angels, principalities, powers; beings on earth—men, kingdoms, empires; beings under the earth—the denizens of the invisible world." This is universal subjection to Christ. We need to remember that universal subjection does not necessarily mean universal salvation.

Consecration to the Ministry

The last words of this last verse of Isaiah 53 really give us a recapitulation of the teaching of the whole chapter concerning the ministry of our Lord. "He hath poured out His soul unto death: and He was numbered with the transgressors; and He bare the sin of many, and made intercession for the transgressors."

When Jesus Christ "cometh into the world, He

saith, Lo, I come to do Thy will, O God." As a lad of twelve He declared that He must be about His Father's business, and in the Garden just preceding His death He declared: "Not My will, but Thine be done." His whole life was consecrated to the great task assigned Him by the Father—the work of our redemption. His exaltation, of which we have just written, was only because He was able to truly say: "I have finished the work which Thou gavest Me to do" (John 17:3). We shall now look at the four-fold statement of His matchless ministry:

"He hath poured out His soul unto death." His "soul" here means His life blood. The blood is the seat of life. "The life is in the blood" (Lev. 17:11). When He poured out His soul He poured out His life, to the last drop. According to Delitzsch the word rendered *poured out* means *to strip, lay bare, empty,* or to *pour clean out,* even to the very last remnant. His blood was completely emptied out "unto death." We believe that the type of the Paschal Lamb must be perfectly fulfilled in Christ, even to the minutest detail. The Passover Lamb was slain according to the Levitical method of severing the soft tissues of the neck with one sweep of the knife, which resulted in immediate and almost painless death and perfect exsanguination of the tissues, the animal being hung head down, so that gravity would favor the flow of blood and its more complete expulsion. The Jew has never used, either for sacrifice or for food, the bodies of animals that have not been rendered as far as possible bloodless. This is what took place when Christ "poured out His soul unto death." "Without the shedding of blood there is no remission of sins," is the testimony of God from one end of His Book to the other. The word "shed" means to *pour forth, to flow, to gush out*—a free, abundant, copious flow of blood. This was the shedding of blood that John saw when our Lord's side was pierced with the spear of the Roman soldier. From the side of the first Adam came Eve—physical life; from the side of

the last Adam came blood—spiritual life, for redemption and regeneration have their source in His sacrifice. All the blood that He could possibly shed was "poured out" for us. His sacrifice was perfect, absolute, abundant, complete. He Himself said, "This is My blood, which is shed for many for the remission of sins."

> "For my cleansing this I see—
> Nothing but the blood of Jesus;
> For my pardon this my plea—
> Nothing but the blood of Jesus."

His voluntary act in death is indicated here. No man could take His life from Him. He laid it down of Himself, even as He took it up again (John 10: 17, 18). When He was in the "form of God" He emptied Himself of His glory, and when He was in "fashion as a man," He emptied out His soul. We are saved because He gave Himself for us. His life was not taken; His life was given. Had man been able to murder Him, Christ could not have been God; Christ is God, hence man was unable to take His life. Murder was in the heart of men when they nailed Him to the Cross; salvation was in the heart of Christ when He suffered them to nail Him there.

"He was numbered with the transgressors." He was not a transgressor, but He was treated as such. "He suffered Himself to be reckoned with transgressors," or "He allowed Himself to be counted among transgressors," is the meaning. He submitted to this indignity that He might save the transgressors. Our Lord directly quoted these words, just before His crucifixion, applying the prophecy to Himself (Luke 22:37). He was numbered with transgressors in life and death. He was born of the virgin Mary, but was counted by His enemies among those born out of wedlock. "We be not born of fornication," the Jews taunted Him—so He was numbered among the transgressors. He was born at Bethlehem, and registered there among the Jewish

people by the command of Caesar, for Israel because
of her sins suffered the yoke of Rome—so He was
numbered among the transgressors. He was called
"that deceiver," "a wine-bibber," a "glutton," a
"friend of publicans and sinners," "this fellow," in
contempt—so He was numbered among the transgressors. He was condemned as a "blasphemer" by
His judges, and crucified by Rome under the charge
of sedition—so He was numbered among the transgressors. He was nailed to the Cross between two
malefactors, or robbers, and His grave was appointed
with the wicked in His death—so He was numbered
with the transgressors.

But He was not only numbered among the transgressors by men: He was also numbered among them
by God; yea, much more, He was counted by God as
the Transgressor, for when Christ went to the Cross,
Jehovah laid on Him the iniquity of us all. He became the world's sinner. God dealt with the One as
if He merited the judgment of the many. He was
smitten and afflicted of God. Jesus Christ yielded
Himself to take the sinner's position. He was numbered with the transgressors that the transgressors
might be numbered with saints.

"He bare the sin of many." "He bare our sins
in His own body on the tree." The Cambridge Bible
notes this clause as "whereas He bare," stating that
this sets forth the true view of His death as op-
posed to the false judgment of men. No matter what
view man takes of the death of Christ, the fact remains that He "was made sin for us," "enduring the
penalty due to it on our behalf, that we might be
freed from the accursed load and 'become the righteousness of God in Him'," writes Baron. This only
is the meaning of the infinite agony of the Son of
God when He was on the accursed tree. This only is
the meaning of that terrible cry that pulsated from
His innermost being, "My God, My God, why hast
Thou forsaken Me?" His sense of separation from
God had its roots in the separation which sin has

effected between man and God. He was the Suffering Soul of our sin-stricken humanity. Certainly nothing could be clearer than the Scriptural statements that Christ "bare our sins."

"The torrents of His passion deep and fierce on Him
    did roll,
And the rivers of transgression overwhelmed His
    human soul.
Sins unknown, sins unimagined, sins by day and
    sins by night,
Sins of blackest outer darkness pressed upon His
    purest sight.
Sins since o'er the Eastern portal first the cherub
    waved his sword,
To the last that shall be written ere the coming of
    the Lord!"

"He made intercession for the transgressors."

Baron says: "The verb, 'made intercession,' is an instance of the imperfect or indefinite future, and expresses a work begun, but not yet ended." Delitzsch observes that its most striking fulfillment was the prayer of the crucified Savior, "Father, forgive them, for they know not what they do." But this did not end His work of intercession, for He now appears at the throne of grace in our behalf. "He ever liveth to make intercession for us." The office which He began on the Cross He now continues in heaven. Alexander says, "Intercession, not in the restricted sense of prayer for others, but in the wider sense of meritorious and prevailing intervention, which is ascribed to Christ in the New Testament, not as a work already finished, like that of atonement, but as still going on (Rom. 8:34; Heb. 9:24; I John 2:1), for which cause the prophet here employs the future form."

Think of what that intercession means for us! What an amazing thing—that the Son of God should intercede for us! We shall never know until we meet Him face to face, how He has interceded for us. We shall never know until then how much we have escaped, of accident and assault, of trial and trouble, of sickness and suffering, of disease and death. That intercession means our preservation, for no one of those who has trusted in Him has ever perished, or ever will perish.

His priestly intercession for the believer is on the basis of the blood shed on the Cross. If Jesus Christ had not died for us He could not intercede for us. Had He not gone to the Cross for us, He could not enter the Court for us. Had He not met the claims of Divine justice against us, He could not meet the accusations of the Adversary against us. Had He not taken our sins upon His body on the tree, He would not dare take our names upon His lips in the glory. In Psalm 16:4, God is speaking of those who reject Him, and declares that He will not "take up their names into My lips." That "He ever liveth to make intercession" is true, but the same verse makes it plain that that intercession is only for those "that come unto God by Him" (Heb. 7:25). Sinner, what an awful thing to think that after Christ loved you enough to die in your stead, your own rejection of Him keeps your name off His lips. Will you not just now follow the suggestion of this verse: "As many as received Him, to them gave He power to become the sons of God, even to them that believe on His name"? Then you will be able to rejoice with all saints that your name is upon His lips in intercession, that your case is in His sure hands.

> "This, my rock, my sure defense,
>   Jesus pleads for me;
> This my ground of confidence,
>   Jesus pleads for me;
> Holy hands that wrought but good—
> Stained with sacrificial blood,
> Lifted, now, in prayer to God,
>   Jesus pleads for me."